HIDDEN HISTORY
of
HOWARD COUNTY

HIDDEN HISTORY

of

HOWARD COUNTY

Nathan S. Davis and Wayne S. Davis

THE
History
PRESS

Published by The History Press
Charleston, SC
www.historypress.com

Front cover: *Baltimore and Ohio Railroad Records, Archives Center, National Museum of American History, Smithsonian Institution.*

First published 2023

Manufactured in the United States

ISBN 9781467154734

Library of Congress Control Number: 2023938418

CONTENTS

Preface

Introduction

There is quite a lot of hidden history in Howard County (HoCo), and in preparation for this book, it sometimes felt like history was being hidden from us. Howard County is the wealthiest county in Maryland and the sixth-wealthiest county in the country, according to a 2022 U.S. News and World Report publication. It sits about halfway between the Baltimore and Washington metropolitan areas, its residents feeding heavily into government agencies at Fort George G. Meade and in Washington, D.C. Our family moved here from Chicago in 1992 because of one opportunity in this wealth of opportunities.

Personal

We started looking at the history of Guilford over six years ago, prompted by an old bridge over the Little Patuxent River and the piles of odd-shaped stones along the adjacent pathways. Walking on the trails in our neighborhood, we would cross over an old iron bridge neither of us knew anything about. There were some signs near the bridge that discussed the quarries that used to be in this area, how railroads were used to ship heaps of stone dug out of the ground to destinations unknown. Neither of us knew much about this local history, but we knew we had found our next project.

We uncovered an abandoned cemetery from the 1800s, just a few hundred feet from the bridge and tucked between a highway and an industrial park. Unearthing these gravestones, as well as stories of Savage, Ellicott City and other places in HoCo that were not always founded in fact, pushed us to publish this book.

Our hidden history search expanded beyond Guilford, as reflected in these pages, but Guilford serves as a microcosm of the county's experience, a community as old as any in Howard that benefitted from ample waterpower for mills, an abundance of prime granite, fertile farmland and the Baltimore and Ohio Railroad.

The stories of Guilford are not isolated from those of the rest of the county, as this was both the social and political center of the county in earlier times. Some readers might open this book and ask, "Why isn't there more information on Ellicott City? Or on the western part of the county?" The answer is simple: we did not set out to write that book. If this book is successful, we intend to follow it up with *Hidden History of Howard County, Part 2*, which will dive more into the county farther out from Guilford.

We feel that history is being hidden from our communities and this book is a start to create more understanding about the past.

Join us as we reveal hidden histories from HoCo and the Guilford area, and we hope you find some of your own, no matter where you live.

History is hidden all around you.

Statement of Purpose

Like most areas south of the Mason-Dixon line, HoCo was built by the enslavement of others, as you will find out in this book. Many of the founding families, lauded for their ingenuity and work ethic, had constructed a foundation on the exploited backs of others. Racism didn't stop with emancipation, as Jim Crow laws and segregation were strongly supported in the county. Our schools were among the last in Maryland to be legally desegregated, with the Guilford Elementary School being the only formerly all-Black school open for all students today. We should not hide this history but factually research it and teach it, so others know it is part of history, past and present.

Acknowledgements

We would like to thank the following people and their organizations, where appropriate, for their support, inspiration and research assistance.

Clara Gouin, retired planner from HoCo Recreation and Parks, paved the way for our initial efforts in early 2017 along with Gerald Ueckermann, Adam Fracchia (University of Maryland) and Johnny Johnsson (Vulcan Materials).

We are grateful to so many others, including Julie Schablitsky and her team from State Highway Administration (now with the Maryland Department of Transportation); Robert Mosko, Tina Simmons and Dennis Green from Coalition to Protect Maryland Burial Sites; Mary Ellen Grady and Sue Mentzler along with Tank and Jax from Chesapeake Search Dogs; Erin Berry with Columbia Archives; Marlena Jareaux with HoCo Lynching Truth & Reconciliation Inc.; local history experts Fred Dorsey, Bessie Bordenave and Ken Short; emeritus historian Robert Vogel for his time educating us about the location of the first Bollman Bridge; and emeritus historian John McGrain for his time educating us on the recent history of Guilford Mill.

The encouragement and assistance from historian Ralph Eshelman, Joan Carter-Smith and the Carter family, Patricia and Austin Platz and Barb and Liam Fuller meant everything.

Jody Frey taught us how to map land patents, and her online Emporium of Amazing Knowledge provides the most accurate electronic files for mapping HoCo and Anne Arundel County (AACo) early land patents.

The help of many staff members at the Maryland State Archives as well as their online public collection was greatly appreciated. The Howard County

Library System allowed access to much information, including its microfiche collection. The Howard County Historical Society Inc. also provided access to its collection.

A special thanks to Gerald Ueckermann for his research skills, including the first timeline for the Guilford Mills, information on the origin of Guilford's name and key elements of the biography of John Savage.

Inevitably, there are names we forgot to include, and we hope for forgiveness.

Of course, we would never have been able to begin or complete this book without the love and support (and editorial review) of our wives, Noelle Davis and Ellen Lathrop-Davis.

Abbreviations

AACo: Anne Arundel County
B&O: Baltimore and Ohio Railroad Company
BoE: Board of Education
EC: Ellicott City
HoCo: Howard County
HCPL: Howard County Public Library
HCPSS: Howard County Public School System
   ES: elementary school, grades K–5
   MS: middle school, grades 6–8
   HS: high school, grades 9–12
MCHC: Maryland Center for History and Culture
MSA: Maryland State Archives
PBR: Patuxent Branch Rail
SMC: Savage Manufacturing Company

Chapter 1

HOWARD COUNTY'S HIDDEN HISTORY

Howard County (HoCo) is located in the geographic center of Maryland, the only one of its counties that is not bordering the Chesapeake Bay or another state.

HoCo is the sixth most populated county and the fourth fastest growing population in Maryland, with about 335,000 people as of this writing. HoCo itself or the "towns" within it, such as Columbia and Ellicott City, have consistently been at the top of "best places to live" rankings.[1]

HoCo contains hidden history waiting to be revealed. While not wanting to reveal its hidden history for fear of damaging its reputation, or perhaps just wanting to move on from its past, some entities in HoCo carefully control its historical narrative to focus on heritage history, whether true or not, whether paved over by Columbia or left to deteriorate along county roads. There is more to HoCo's history than the arrival of the Ellicott brothers along the Patapsco River in 1772, although it seems that most who deal with HoCo history would rather begin the story there. Let's start with the first European settlements in HoCo and who likely lived here before land patents were issued to the settlers.

THE FIRST SETTLEMENTS

Any mention of the first European settlements in HoCo must be coupled with acknowledgement of those who were here before any European colonists arrived. The relationships among Indigenous peoples and their

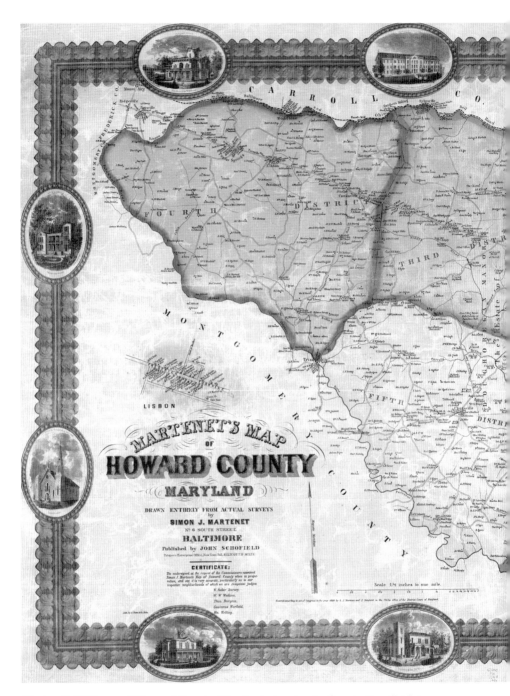

Martenet's 1860 map of Howard County, Maryland, showing the five election districts. *Library of Congress.*

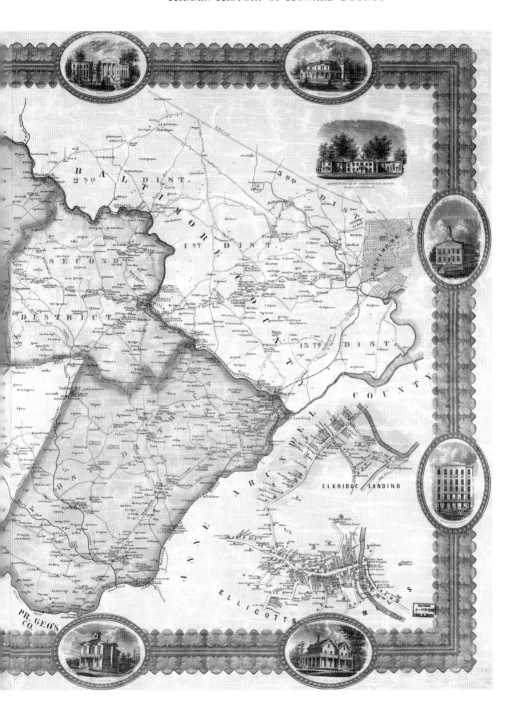

many tribes were complex. Captain John Smith's 1612 map prominently featured the Powhatan Confederacy, which was composed of perhaps dozens of Algonquian peoples tribes, including the Piscataway tribe as well as the Susquehannock, an Iroquoian peoples tribe.[2] There is still academic debate over some of these groupings, because historic documents did not focus on Indigenous peoples and were certainly not written from their viewpoint.

It is generally accepted that HoCo is on the territorial lands of the Susquehannock and Piscataway Tribes.[3] In 2012, the State of Maryland recognized the Piscataway Indian Nation "stretching from the Appalachian Mountains to the shores of the Chesapeake Bay and Atlantic Ocean."[4] In 2020, the University of Maryland, Baltimore County (UMBC), located less than two miles from HoCo, offered the following land acknowledgement, which we would like to share as we believe it to also be applicable to this book:

> *UMBC was established upon the land of the Piscataway and Susquehannock peoples. Over time, citizens of many more Indigenous nations have come to reside in this region. We humbly offer our respect to all past, present, and future Indigenous people connected to this place.*[5]

While it is difficult to determine the exact boundaries defined by a 1652 treaty between the Susquehannock and the Maryland colonial government, they extended along the Chesapeake's western shore between the Patuxent River and Garrett Island in the Susquehanna River near Havre de Grace.[6] Did these boundaries extend into HoCo? We just don't have a definitive understanding of the extent of the Susquehannock lands, including how far upstream they went or whether they included both sides of the Patuxent River. We do know that the northern and southern boundaries followed two rivers with names of Indigenous origin: Patapsco (either "ledge of rock" or "backwater") and Patuxent ("at the little rapids or falls in a stream").[7]

Owning land in Maryland's early colonial days required (1) a warrant issued by a government official to the county surveyor documenting the acres of land through a certificate of survey, (2) a detailed survey of the land with a scale drawing of the tracts of land of interest and adjacent properties and (3) a patent for the land that was not already patented.[8] Land surveys and patents established the metes and bounds of property that passed from one generation, or owner, to another. Many property records through the 1800s still identified the earlier land patents, which provided a fairly easy way of determining the location of a specific tract of land.

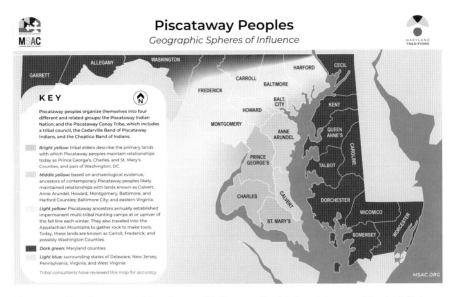

Piscataway Peoples geographic spheres of influence. *Land Acknowledgements, Maryland State Arts Council.*

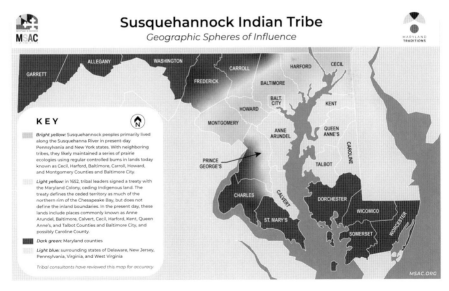

Susquehannock Indian Tribe geographic spheres of influence. *Land Acknowledgements, Maryland State Arts Council.*

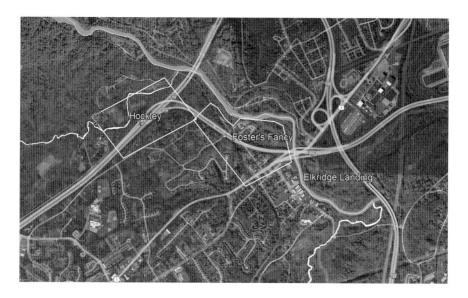

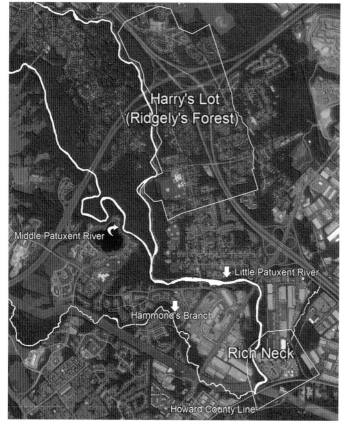

Above: Earliest HoCo land patents, Hockley and Foster's Fancy. *Author's collection.*

Left: Earliest land patents in southeast HoCo, Rich Neck and Ridgely's Forest. *Author's collection.*

The first land patents granted to colonists within the modern boundaries of HoCo were along the Patapsco River to the north and the Patuxent River to the south. Waterways were critical features, providing not only potable water but also power for the earliest mills, built along fall lines. On the northern boundary of what was then Anne Arundel County, Joseph Foster, a local farmer, patented one hundred acres of land on the south side of the Patapsco River called Fosters Fancy in 1670, the same year that William Ebden patented a one-hundred-acre area called Hockley.[9] These lands were near what would become Elk Ridge Landing.

The southern boundary of the county included Major General John Hammond's 1684 patent Rich Neck, along the Little Patuxent River at the mouth of Hammond's Branch, as well as Colonel Henry Ridgely's 1686 patent called Ridgely's Forrest, covering much of today's Guilford area "lying on the east side of the North Great Branch of Patuxent River at Huntington."[10] These early patents started the western settlements of HoCo.

When Howard County Was in Baltimore County

Was HoCo once a part of Baltimore County? This possibility is mentioned in an excellent booklet written by Vera Ruth Filby and published by the Savage Civic Association in 1965 titled *Savage, Maryland*. Filby writes that the land patents of Wincopin Neck and Harry's Lott "were part of what was then Baltimore County, and had been since 1659. In 1726 they became part of Anne Arundel County."[11] HoCo officially came from the northwest portion of Anne Arundel County in 1851, but was there this previous connection with Baltimore County?[12]

In 1907, Edward B. Mathews's *The Counties of Maryland: Their Origins, Boundaries, and Election Districts* was published.[13] This authoritative source on county boundaries in Maryland answers when and where the boundary was established between Anne Arundel and Baltimore Counties in 1698–1727. Mathews's book provides a clear justification for including Guilford and Savage within Baltimore County.

Mathews writes that in 1696, Maryland commissioners had the task of establishing the boundary between Baltimore and Anne Arundel Counties, and two years later, Chapter 13 of the Acts of 1698 was enacted into Maryland law. Mathews quotes the pertinent section of the Acts in his book but notes that few of the mapping points in the narrative were still able to be located when his book was published. However,

> *the intention was to place the boundary along the divide between the Magothy and the Patapsco rivers as far as Elk Ridge, and thence westerly to the Patuxent in such a way as to include all of the settlements then made. This would make the line indefinite and would extend at that time just north of the present location of the Baltimore and Ohio Railroad. Grants had just been given to large tracts in the vicinity of Savage and Guilford, and along Warfield's Ridge.*[14]

Mathews seems to answer the question in the affirmative of whether Guilford and Savage were actually at one time in Baltimore County. But there was one more question: Where in Elk Ridge was the dividing point? Simon Martenet provides that answer in a unique map done in 1865, just after the Civil War.[15] That map displays Maryland, the District of Columbia and portions of Virginia and Delaware. One special aspect of this map is the drawing of the "Old Baltimore County Line."

Martenet shows the Baltimore County line beginning south of the mouth of the Patapsco River, going west-southwest to south of Annapolis Junction to an area called "Three Marked Pines." From this point to the west, where

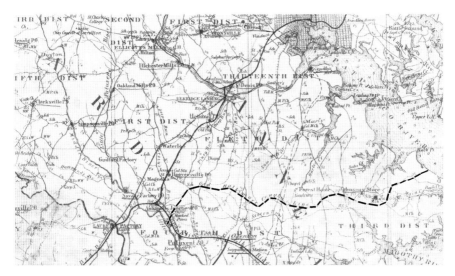

Martenet's 1865 map of Maryland showing the "Old Baltimore County Line" and the boundaries of old Baltimore County. *Library of Congress.*

G.M. Hopkins Atlas of Howard County, 1878. *Johns Hopkins Sheridan Libraries.*

an imaginary line would meet the Patuxent River at Laurel, the map would basically include the borders of HoCo.

But where did the border go from there? Chapter 13 of the Acts of April 3, 1698, had a detailed description: once the border met at the Patuxent River, it went

> *up the said River to the Extent thereof for the Bounds of Baltemore* [sic] *County.…All that Tract of Land lying on the north side of the said Division lines trees…are to be in Baltemore County and all the Lands and Inhabitants…on the South side of the said Lines Trees and land marks to the ancient extent of Ann Arundell* [sic] *County…and be in Ann Arundel County.*[16]

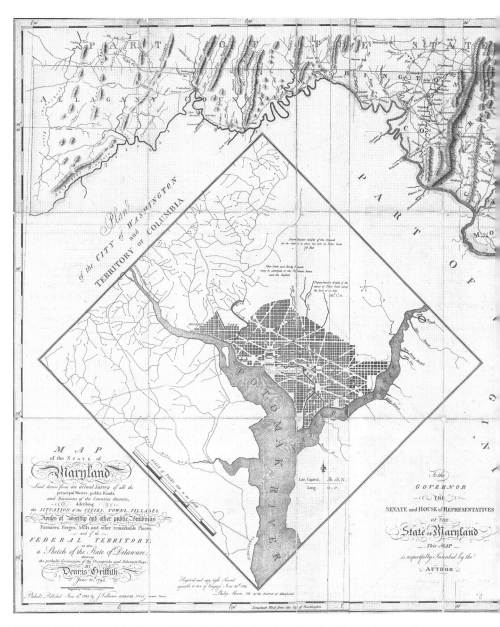

Griffith's 1794 map of the State of Maryland, showing Ann Arundel County boundaries. *Library of Congress.*

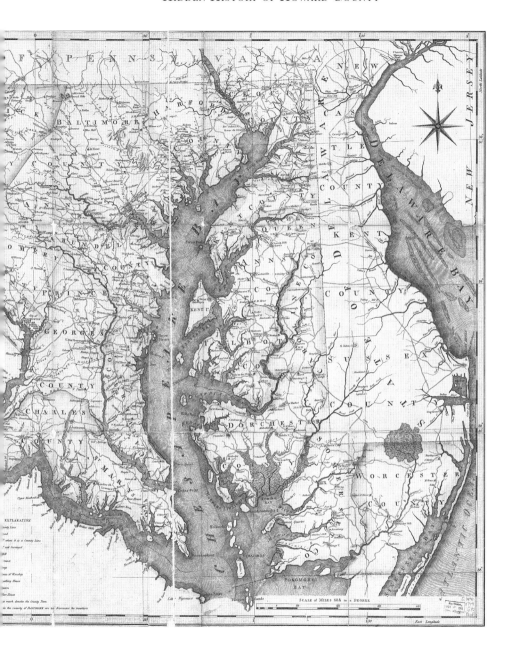

The Patuxent River traveled northwest to approximately what is now Mount Airy, where the headwaters of the Patuxent and Patapsco Rivers once met, according to Griffith's 1794 map.

This gives the full picture that basically all of current-day HoCo was indeed once part of Baltimore County. In 1726, the state legislature reversed the boundary back to the Patapsco River—effective January 7, 1727—as the southern border of Baltimore County, which is the current boundary.[17] This information is useful when researching records of the 1698–1726 era, since it changes what records and terms to search for. It seems that Filby was correct and Guilford, Savage and nearly all of HoCo was actually part of Baltimore County for almost thirty years.

Elk Ridge Landing

Elk Ridge Landing is and was located along the Patapsco River near Deep Run and the Falls of the Patapsco. In the 1700s, it was a key seaport and trade center where local farmers, millers and others could bring their goods (mostly tobacco, at the time) to be shipped overseas and also receive goods.[18]

"Ridge of Elks" is cited by historian Joetta Cramm as the origin of the name Elkridge, and while this is a plausible origin, no original source of information is provided.[19] The first record found of the phrase "ridge of elk(s)" for this area was in Warfield (1905); a subsequent record appears in a 1937 book by Robert Schnepfe Diggs called *The Early History of Elkridge Landing*.[20]

Certificates of survey issued to Joseph Foster in 1670 for "Foster's Fancy" and to William Ebden for "Hockley" are the first ones issued for the land that is now seen as Elk Ridge Landing, but there is no mention of the name Elk Ridge in these certificates.[21] Foster's Fancy was mentioned in the certificate for Hockley and was just downstream of Hockley along the Patapsco next to what would become Elk Ridge Landing. The name Elk Ridge appears by 1687 in a land certificate granted to Adam Shipley called "Adam the First" with five hundred acres "on a Ridge called Elkridge."[22] During this period, it appears additional settlement was occurring and the role of Elk Ridge Landing as a key tobacco port was firmly established.[23]

In March 1733, the Maryland General Assembly enacted a law called "An Act for Erecting a Town at and about the landing, called, The Elk-Ridge Landing, near the Head of Potapsco [sic] River, in Anne Arundel County."[24] Thirty acres of land was to be included, laid out in forty lots, and

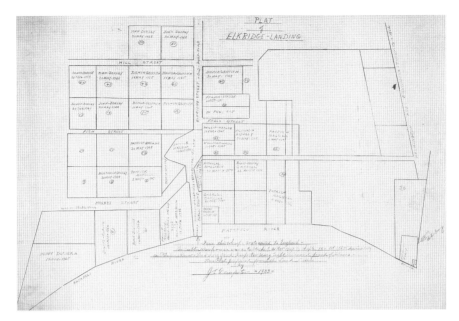

Plat of Elkridge Landing from 1700s land records by J.E. Dempster in 1933. *MSA.*

the settlement was to be called Jansen-Town, but it was never established because authority to create it lapsed. Elk Ridge Landing was still the port where tobacco and other goods were brought to be shipped to England and vice versa.

By the 1750s, the navigation of the Patapsco River to Elk Ridge Landing was in danger. This prompted the legislature to pass an "Act to prevent injuring the navigation to Baltimore-town, and to the inspecting house at Elk-Ridge Landing, on Patapsco River" on November 17, 1753. Part of the problem addressed was "that by opening and digging into the banks of the Patapsco River for iron stone, large quantities of earth and land are thrown and washed into the said river...by which practice (if continued), the channel of the said river, and navigable branches...will, in a short time, be so filled up" that navigation would not be possible.[25] This was, apparently, the fate of the river.

In 1825, nine of the ten houses in Elkridge Landing were destroyed by fire. The *Niles Weekly Register* reported that the "time is perfectly within the memory of persons, not very aged, when this landing, on the Patapsco, was expected one day to be what Baltimore is—a great city."[26] It may not have become a great city, but it was an important early community in HoCo.

Guilford

The Guilford area is in southeastern HoCo and is mostly covered by seven original land patents, described below. Based on these land surveys and patents, we can say that the Guilford-Savage area was first settled about 1686 and the first mill, a gristmill, was likely operating in current-day Savage by 1726. The early land patents for the Guilford area include Ridgely's Forrest/Harry's Lott, Wincopin Neck, Jones Fancy, Hall's Lott, Warfield's Contrivance and White's Fortune/White's Contrivance.[27]

An act was passed on October 24, 1728, to form the new Queen Caroline Parish in Anne Arundel County from parts of All-Hallows and St. Anne's Parishes, essentially covering much of the land of current day HoCo.[28] The main church serving this parish was Christ Episcopal Church, also known as the Christ Church of Guilford, which became HoCo's first true social center. The church vestry oversaw collecting tobacco and other taxes from the residents of the parish, among other things. The vestry members, as of November 1728, were Thomas Wainwright; John Dorsey, son of Edward; John Hammond, son of Charles; Orlando Griffith; Richard Davis; and Robert Shipley.[29] To manage outreach and collections, especially the counting of tobacco plants, the church established precincts that eventually gave way to the Hundreds designation for Patuxent, Huntington, Elkridge and Bare Ground Hundreds for the parish.[30]

The "Town of Guilford" historical marker[31] indicates "the name 'Guilford' may have come from the town of Guildford in Surrey, England, known for its textiles, or it may commemorate Lord Guilford, the guardian of Charles, the fifth Lord Baltimore." The first appearance we found of the name Guilford in HoCo was in the June 5, 1789 indenture of Richard Ridgely to John Conman to pay off some debts.[32] The tracts of land he bartered were collectively called Guilford and included parts of, or the whole of, eight separate land patents totaling 1,393 acres, although no other record of such a tract or patent has yet been found. In 1792, Richard Stringer deeded several properties to Archibald Moncrief, a Baltimore merchant, including all those lands and mills called the "Guilford Mills."[33] Richard Stringer first owned the Guilford Mills with Richard Ridgely in 1785 and likely named the mills when they were purchased.[34]

Guilford Mills was likely named for the Battle of Guilford Courthouse, which took place in North Carolina in 1781, during the Revolutionary War, just four years before Stringer purchased the mills. After the battle, the Maryland regiments famous for "holding the line" in critical battles

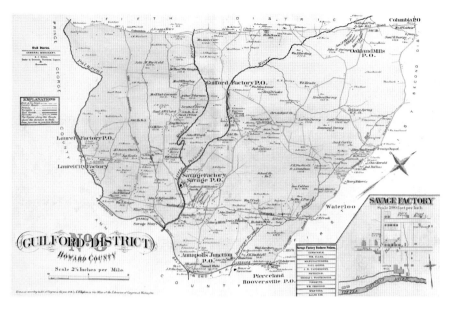

G.M. Hopkins Atlas of Guilford Election District No. 6, 1878. *Johns Hopkins Sheridan Libraries.*

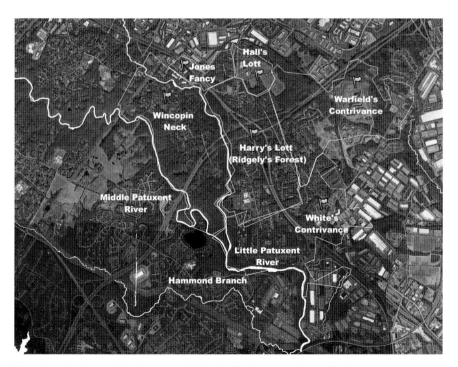

Map showing the early land patents of the Guilford area. *Author's collection.*

were widely recognized and honored.[35] The phrase is so famous that it appeared on the Maryland state quarter, released by the U.S. Mint in 1999. Richard Stringer, co-owner of Guilford Mills, served as a captain in the Maryland regiments from 1776 through 1782, much of that time under Colonel Thomas Dorsey.[36] Stringer either served at the Battle of Guilford Courthouse or knew friends who fought and died in that battle. The Guilford neighborhood in Baltimore was also named to honor those Marylanders who fought in the Battle of Guilford Courthouse.[37]

Early Post Offices

The history of some towns begins with their post offices. Post offices literally put towns on the map, as they became well-known centers for news, business and personal mail. Guilford's was an indication of business success, first from the cotton mill and then from the quarries. "Guilford" already had some history as the name of HoCo's Election District Six.[38]

According to U.S. Postal Service records, the Guilford Post Office opened on December 31, 1874, with Stephen P. Heath, then the proprietor of the Guilford Mills, being the first postmaster. (Frederick) August Brunner, a local farmer, took over as postmaster on August 29, 1888, and kept that position until February 1909.[39] During that time, Brunner purchased the 160-acre Guilford Mills site from new owner James A. Gary in 1894, four years after the mill burned down.[40]

On February 27, 1909, Andrew Kirkpatrick, who was affiliated as a contractor with the local quarries—including the Howard Granite Company and the Guilford Granite Company—became the local postmaster. Jason A. Lawrence, Arthur H. Gillis, Samuel Morningstar and John R. Tipton were the other postmasters of Guilford until June 30, 1920, when the post office of Guilford was moved to "Jessups."[41]

The demise of the Guilford post office coincided with the end of the granite quarry business. The post office was last located in the Guilford General Store, which was just west of the old elementary school near the corner of Oakland Mills and Guilford Roads.

Ellicott's Mills, as Ellicott City was known until 1867, had a post office as early as April 1, 1798, with Samuel Godfrey as postmaster.[42] Savage had a post office, which opened on January 13, 1836, once the Washington Branch Rail Road came close enough to provide mail delivery and pickup. The Savage Manufacturing Company agent, Amos A. Williams, served as

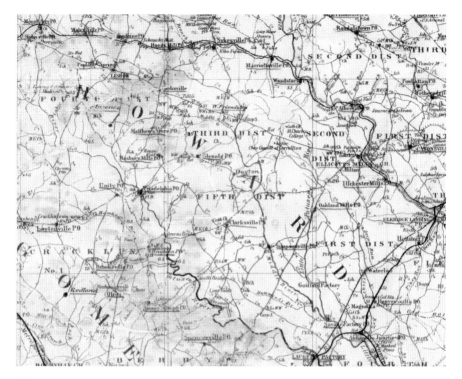

Martenet's 1865 map, showing HoCo post offices (underlined). *Library of Congress.*

postmaster.[43] Oakland Mills was operating by June 30, 1823, with Charles Mathews and Richard Stockett as postmasters. Elk Ridge Landing had a post office by October 12, 1825, operated by John Blue. Even Cooksville, a western HoCo town farther from the railroad and Baltimore metropolis, had an early start at establishing a post office, around July 15, 1824, with Larkin S. Cook as postmaster.[44]

THE FORGOTTEN HOWARD COUNTIAN—COLOR ME BLACK

Beulah (Meacham) Buckner (1930–2005) was a researcher and historian of African American history in HoCo.[45] She was motivated to document Black history through discovering and recording historic schools, churches and cemeteries and researching government records and genealogy documenting the Black communities that existed in an area now bulldozed and developed into Columbia. Buckner knew it was crucial to publicly record this hidden and disappearing history as an important component of HoCo's past, present and future. She intended that her meticulous research from the 1980s and 1990s would culminate in a book called *The Forgotten Howard Countian—Color Me Black*.[46]

In her unpublished work, she wrote:

> *I found that these Historical Society and Individual Howard County historians have been content to borrow Frederick Douglass from Talbot County, Harriett Tubman from Dorchester County, Benjamin Banneker from Baltimore County, and Mathew Henson from Charles County whenever reporting African American contributions to Howard County or the State of Maryland, as if these four great African Americans were the sum total of the African American intelligence and contributions in Maryland. Howard County is particularly guilty of the omission by including Benjamin Banneker in their history when he actually lived in Baltimore County and worked in Ellicott City in Howard County. Rather than take the time to document the history of those African Americans who were born in and made contributions to the history of Howard County.*
>
> *These records provided information that from the beginning of the county both Free Blacks and Slaves helped build the roads, worked in the quarries, iron works and mills; tilled the land, fought in their wars and helped raise the children of those elegant white families while they were busy being elegant. They also showed that the great manors of Howard County, which Howard County white society is always so proud to possess and talk about but quick to forget and seldom mention that Free Blacks and Slaves provided most of the labor in the building of these manors and beautiful gardens surrounding them.*[47]

The collection of Beulah Buckner's work has been in the possession of the HoCo government since her passing in 2005. We hope that it will be fully catalogued and digitized to become available to the public. The quality and quantity of records Buckner obtained are impressive, containing documents, journals, newspaper clippings, notes, typed pages of her manuscript, computer disks, photos, slide negatives and more. Her research is overwhelming and powerful, especially knowing how she felt about the lack of research into our county's Black history. The information she collected is still difficult to find today. We hope that the small steps taken in this book to bring attention to her work will facilitate a deeper look into this hidden and remarkable history.

Chapter 2

FALLS AND GRISTMILLS

O ne of the unique features of our area is the many river and stream rapids that are created as the hilly Piedmont ecoregion changes into the flat coastal plain. The "fall line" of this boundary is filled with sharp changes in elevation creating powerful rapids, which are ready-made power sources for mills. Fortunately, the late Baltimore historian and Maryland molinographer, or mill historian, John McGrain provided his many years of work for online access in 2007.[48]

Howard County became a well-known location of different types of mills. Gristmills, or flour mills, grind wheat and grain into flour and middlings to be used for the base of food consumption for humans and domesticated animals. Cotton mills housed spinning or weaving machinery to produce yarn or cloth from picked cotton, which could, in turn, be used in textile mills to make clothing, sails and other goods. Sawmills cut logs into lumber, uniform sizes and lengths of wood, to be used in building any wood structure; sawmills were typically the first mills erected on a site, producing lumber from which all other sites would be built.

THE FIRST MILL

One of the first gristmills in the HoCo region, almost one hundred years before Savage Mill and fifty years before Ellicott's Mills, was White's Mill. Joseph White already owned and operated Proctors Mill along Broad Creek in Annapolis, so he was well prepared to do the same along the great falls

Map showing land patents of White's Mill Land and Barney's Mill Race in current-day Savage. *Author's collection.*

of the Little Patuxent in what became Savage. Surveyed in 1726, White's Fortune, containing 268 acres, was patented in 1734 for Joseph White Sr. The 1726 survey mentioned a Millrace belonging to White, indicating a mill was already on-site. The survey stated White's Fortune was "standing by the head of a small Race belonging to the said White standing by the Great Dam of Stones and near the Great Falls of Patuxent River."[49]

J.D. Warfield, a prominent HoCo researcher, wrote that Joseph White was a descendent of Peregrine White, the first White child born in Massachusetts after the *Mayflower* landed.[50] However, a deeper dive into research could not find a link between the two or any members of the White family originating in Maryland.[51]

The mill continued operation after Joseph White's death in 1733. In 1752, Joseph White Jr. patented eight and a half acres called Mill Land that appeared to have been unclaimed by others.[52] This land was in a critical location where the Savage Mill dam would eventually be built. White's Fortune was surveyed again in 1759, when the Marlborough Plains land patent and a great amount of vacant lands were added to total 801 acres, three times the size of White's Fortune, but it wasn't patented until 1797, by Griffith White, one of the grandsons of Joseph White Sr.[53]

White's Mill operated for decades more, as seen in the 1794 Griffith map.[54] But after Joseph White Jr. died in 1793, his sons Gideon and Horatio inherited the Mill Land. It is not known how long they may have kept up operations. In January 1823, Gideon sold the Mill Land and much of White's Contrivance to John Savage, the namesake of the town of Savage and its manufacturing company. In this deed, there was no mention of an operating mill.[55] But in the 1850 census, a gristmill making flour, cornmeal and feed was operating in Savage. We wonder if the gristmill advertised for rent in 1851 by the Savage Manufacturing Company (SMC) could have been White's Mill.[56]

GUILFORD MILL

The area between the Little Patuxent and Middle Patuxent Rivers was settled by Richard and Benjamin Warfield in 1702. Children of an immigrant from London, they filed for a patent for Wincopin Neck. Due to a boundary error, the resulting resurveying reduced the original land plot to only 633 acres, which was made up almost in full by adding 231 acres of neighboring vacant land. Also, during the resurveying, Benjamin's name was removed, as he had passed away from illness in 1718.[57]

The first written mention of Guilford Mill dates to 1744, in an agreement between Richard Green and Alexander Warfield, a nephew of Richard and

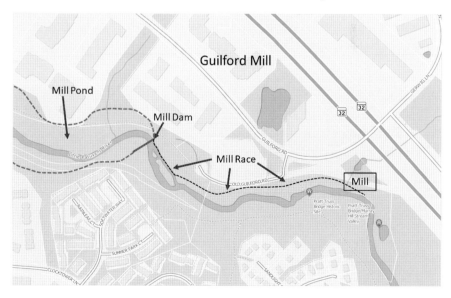

Map showing Guilford Mill, including mill pond, dam, race and mill locations. *Author's collection.*

Benjamin Warfield. This agreement stated that Green and Alexander would build a gristmill with two millstones, one of which was at the mill of Richard Warfield's son, also named Alexander. This agreement stated that "the said Alexander Warfield doth covenant and agree to and with the said Green to find a pair of mill stones that is now one of them at the Indian Landing and the other at Alexander Warfield Son of Richard's mill."[58] Green's mill was on the big Patuxent River near Green's Bridge.

Benjamin Warfield always intended for his only daughter, Elizabeth, to inherit his share of Wincopin Neck when he died. In 1735, when Richard Warfield re-patented the land, it remained in his name. Richard then drafted his own will in 1753 to provide Benjamin's half share to Elizabeth. In October 1761, Alexander (son of Richard) deeded what had originally been Benjamin's half to Elizabeth, so she could complete the sale of her land to Joseph Watson. When Elizabeth sold her share to Joseph Watson, a shoemaker, on April 13, 1761, it must have been revealed that she lacked a proper title to the land, so her cousin, Richard's son Alexander, ensured she got her half through an October 1761 deed formally splitting the land.

Joseph Watson's 1779 will provided his lands, including the mill, to Mary Polton, his wife's daughter. Mary and her husband, John, sold the mill in the 1780s to Richard Ridgely and Richard Stringer. They owned and operated it for a few years and were the first ones to use the name Guilford Mills. Griffith's 1794 map showed that the mill was owned by Richard Owings, who also owned and operated mills later known as the Simpsonville Mills on the Middle Patuxent River. It was Alexander Warfield's son, Dr. Joshua Warfield, who built the mills at Simpsonville. The two Owings Mills locations are discussed a little later in this chapter.

In 1830, James, a son of Richard Owings, took over Guilford Mill from Zachariah Polton and added a cotton mill in about 1833. Its success as a cotton mill wavered, and in the 1850 census of manufacturers, only a gristmill and sawmill owned by another son of Richard Owings, Henry H. Owings, was listed, and no activity was reported in the 1860 census of manufacturing for the mills. In 1867, Owings sold the land to Stephen Heath, a machinist and cotton mill expert, who later obtained a mortgage for the property from James S. Gary, who owned the Alberton Mill in HoCo along the Patapsco River. In 1870, Stephen Heath was the proprietor of both the Guilford and Laurel cotton mills.[59]

In an interesting note, William Baldwin first tried to purchase Guilford Mill in 1845 before he became the owner of Savage Mill in 1859.[60] The Guilford cotton mill operated until it burned down in 1890.[61]

Remains of Guilford milldam, 2018. *Courtesy of Stephen Mangiulli.*

Today, little remains of Guilford Mill. McGrain wrote this about the history of Guilford Mill and a letter he received in February 1976 from L.H. Luckado of Guilford:

> The mill stood about 100 ft below the old B. & O. bridge on the south side of Route 32 and today only one corner of the stone foundation is left to be seen and was first a corn mill and gristmill, then became a cotton mill, then a store, the post office during the quarry days, and then burned. The water wheel is estimated by me to have been 18 to 20 feet high and maybe 50 hp [horsepower], and remains of the dam are ¼ mile upriver, and part can be seen today. There was also a cooper shop that Columbia City just bulldozed down last year.[62]

Upstream there is still an intact 110-foot section of the milldam, more than 150 years old and hidden on Columbia Association open space.

HAMMOND'S LOST MILL

There was once a mill a mile or more downstream from the Guilford Mills. There doesn't appear to be a physical trace remaining of this mill; it is just a lost mill. Traveling along the Patuxent Branch trail upstream of Vollmerhausen Road, imagine a gristmill powered by a millrace and dam operating along the river. With a twenty-five-foot drop of the river from upstream of I95 down toward Vollmerhausen Road, one can perhaps picture that waterpower starting with a dam and a millrace. But exactly where was it located?

In 1771, Charles Greenbury Ridgely Sr., in partnership with Benjamin Griffith and John Hammond, patented a narrow stretch of land on the river called "Mill Seat in Partnership."[63] Part of the land in the Griffith, Ridgely and Hammond partnership included the nine acres of the Mill Seat in Partnership, nine acres on the east of that belonging to Harry's Lott—which would have given room for a millrace and mill—and three acres on the west side of the river (part of Wincopin Neck) that provided some room for the dam and millpond on that side of the river.

In 1777, Benjamin Griffith sold his third to Charles Greenbury Ridgely Jr. who the, with John Hammond, owned half.[64] In 1781, John Hammond sold his share to his son, Nathan.[65] In 1792, after his father's death, Charles

Map showing land patent of Mill Seat in Partnership and surrounding sites along the Little Patuxent River. *Author's collection.*

Greenbury Ridgely Jr. and his mother, Sarah, sold their half interest in the mill and land to Nathan Hammond, giving him full interest in the mill and land—hence the name Hammond's Mill.[66]

Hammond's Mill was just upstream of the Vollmerhausen Road crossing along the Little Patuxent River. In 1797, Nathan Hammond sold his interests in the mill and land to Philip Hammond Hopkins and described the mill as "about a mile or more below the lower mills belonging to Richard Owings Esquire" (a.k.a. Guilford Mills) and containing a "Mill Dam, Mill stones, timbers, Mill Irons, wheels, Rolling Iron & Gears." Hammond also sold "all and every article thing, tool and implement belonging to or appertaining to the said mill, dam, houses, race" and other materials.[67] Hopkins sold the twenty-one-acre mill site to the Savage Manufacturing Company in 1832.[68]

The Ellicott Brothers
and Bartholomew Balderston

Almost fifty years after Joseph White established his gristmill on the Little Patuxent River, an even larger milling operation would take hold along the Patapsco River. This story of the Ellicott brothers, who established the mill lands in the 1770s later known as Ellicott City, presents some little-known aspects of this endeavor that readers may find enlightening.

The initial presence of the Ellicott brothers (Joseph, Andrew, Nathaniel and John), Quakers from Bucks County, Pennsylvania—yes, there was a Nathaniel, who is often forgotten—begins on the Baltimore County side of the Patapsco River in April 1771. They purchased lands from William Teal (fifty acres of Teals Search) and William Williams (thirty-four acres of Mt. Gilboa) that would become known as the lower mills. Ellicott & Co., as they would become known, began building their mills in 1772, and in a short time there was not only a gristmill and sawmill but also a plaster mill and a slitting mill for iron.[69]

Numerous tales exist of the Ellicotts being on the south side of the river in 1772 due to the Maryland Mill Act of 1669, which allowed condemnation of twenty acres of land on each side of a river to benefit whoever would build a gristmill. What few realize was that the Maryland Mill Act was repealed in 1766, resulting in the Ellicotts' eventual land purchases on both sides of the river.[70] But the Ellicotts were not in today's HoCo until the end of 1774.

The Ellicotts' arrival in AACo on the south side of the Patapsco River occurred on December 31, 1774, when they purchased two tracts of land

Map showing land patents of the upper and lower Ellicott's Mills. *Author's collection.*

from miller Benjamin Hood about four miles upstream of the lower mills. The four brothers, along with George Wall Jr. of Bucks County, purchased one 20-acre tract along the Patapsco Falls called Hoods Haven (after James Hood, Benjamin's father) containing a flour and sawmill, with an eighty-year lease from the then governor of the province to "build Water Mills," to encourage construction of mills.[71] They also purchased the 40-acre Baker's Delight and the 115-acre resurveyed Hoods Haven. These were the first lands they bought in AACo.

George Wall Jr. sold his moiety (half share) in the mill site on January 21, 1777, to the four brothers, and a few months later, on April 24, Nathaniel sold his interest in the in the Maryland properties for a farm plantation in Bucks County. In 1778, on June 22, Joseph exchanged his ownership in the lower mills for sole ownership of what was known as the upper mill, where he built his homestead. Joseph died in 1780, and his four sons took over ownership of the lands.[72]

That was quite an adventure in land buying from the Ellicott brothers. But how did the remaining three brothers obtain lands at the lower mills on the HoCo side of the Patapsco River? It turns out that a member of their Quaker Buckingham Meeting in Bucks County, Pennsylvania, likely preceded them to what would become HoCo's Ellicott City.

Bartholomew Balderston was born in Bucks County, Pennsylvania, in 1743 to John and Hannah.[73] Balderston attended the same Friends Buckingham meeting as the Ellicott family. He happened to fall in love with Sarah Johnson, who was not a member of the Society of Friends, and in 1764, Balderston was officially admonished by the Friends meeting for their relationship. After he married her on June 24, 1764, it was determined at the March 4, 1765 Buckingham Monthly Meeting that "Balderston hath accomplished his marriage out of the Unity of Friends with one not of our Society, tho' timely precaution to the contrary by several, and his wife was delivered of a child within less than seven months after marriage." He was no longer welcome.[74]

It is still undetermined exactly when Balderston and his family moved from Pennsylvania to Maryland, but it seems likely to have been shortly after he left the Society of Friends. He moved to the AACo side of the Patapsco River and may have arrived before the Ellicotts. On December 8, 1774, Balderston sold twenty-three acres of Prestiges Folly and seven and a half acres of Good Neighborhood along the Patapsco River to the four Ellicotts, the first lands the brothers would own in what became Ellicott City. It seems these lands were used to house workers associated with the mills.[75]

On May 14, 1796, Balderston sold 0.52 acres of land from his Prestiges Folly for a "burying ground for the Society of the people called Quakers." On July 28, 1796, Jonathan Ellicott and others, all living in Baltimore County, sold 1.6 acres of land, from the 23 acres bought from Balderston, to Benjamin Rich and others living in AACo for a new Elk Ridge Friends Meeting House. Balderston and his family may not have been part of the Society of Friends anymore, but his land provided everything needed to establish Quaker roots in what would become Ellicott's Mills and then Ellicott City. Ironically, his younger brother Isaiah became a minister of the Society of Friends in Baltimore and interacted with the Ellicotts frequently, but there is no evidence of the two brothers meeting each other again. Bartholomew Balderston had died by 1803; the exact date is unknown.

Owings Mills in Howard County

Owings Mills is not just a town in Baltimore County (BaCo).[76] HoCo had our own Owings Mills for over fifty years! Both Owings Mills were related, literally. Samuel Owings Jr. inherited his father's sawmill in 1775 before building at least three mills along Gwynn's Falls in BaCo—an area now known as Owings Mills. Samuel Jr. had a younger brother, Richard, who married Ruth Warfield, the daughter of Dr. Joshua Warfield. Dr. Warfield built and operated mills on the Middle Patuxent River about five miles upstream of White's Mill at Savage. Ironically, it was Dr. Warfield's father,

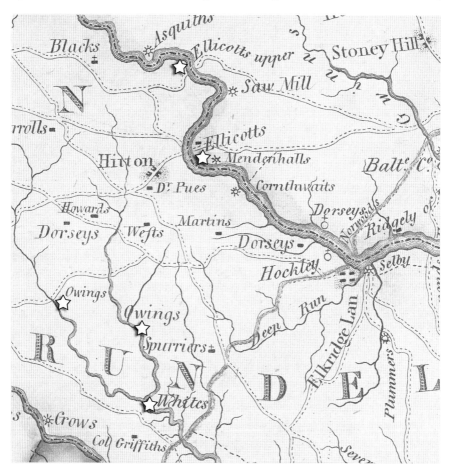

Map of the State of Maryland (1794) by Dennis Griffith showing Owings, White's and Ellicott's Mills. *Library of Congress.*

Alexander (Richard Warfield's son) who built the Guilford Mills on the Little Patuxent just a few miles away. It seems the mill business ran in the family.

By the 1790s, the mills at Guilford and modern-day Simpsonville were both owned by Richard Owings. His family lived near the upper mill, and the area was known as Owingsville. Those mills were purchased by Charles Simpson in 1850, and the area became Simpsonville.

Chapter 3

THE STONE THAT BUILT
HOWARD COUNTY

In Howard County, granite is abundant. Throughout many of its towns and neighborhoods, you may find outcroppings of rock as old as the American continent itself. Granite in HoCo was so geologically significant that the two main types of granite in the area were named after the commercial quarries in Guilford and Ellicott City. The U.S. Geological Survey (USGS) describes "Guilford Quartz Monzonite" as dating back approximately 420 million years and only found in the Guilford and Atholton areas of HoCo, including an area around the Middle Patuxent River. Still, it represents only 1.5 percent of the geological area in the county.

Guilford Granite was privately quarried for building homes in the early 1800s, before it was commercially mined at the Guilford quarries. The Charles Stewart house, called Granite Park, was built with the granite quarried along the Middle Patuxent River upstream of Murray Hill Road.[77] Guilford granite was also used in Savage to improve the Savage Factory Dam and the abutments supporting the original Bollman Bridge.[78]

"Ellicott City Granodiorite" also dates to about 420 million years ago and differs only slightly from the Guilford granite. Ellicott City granite is found in both Baltimore and Howard Counties. Woodstock Granite is another famous area granite, a little darker in color than the Guilford granite, located across the Patapsco River in BaCo. The Guilford, Ellicott City and Woodstock granites made large economic and social impacts on HoCo, as they were used for the B&O Railroad, for building and monument stones and, as crushed stone, for roadbed materials.

Map of the HoCo area showing locations of granite deposits. *HoCo GIS.*

Gabbro is not granite but rather a hard rock with a much darker color and a higher iron content that can appear rusty in color. Like granite, this stone is usually crushed and used for roadbed construction. It is common in the Guilford and Jessup area.[79]

DIGGING PUTNEY AND RIDDLE

True Putney and Hugh Riddle were pioneers in the granite industry in the 1830s. Granite became a focus for wide commercial use due to the need for granite sills to fasten the iron track onto for the early B&O Railroad.[80] Putney and Riddle were among those selling granite sills for the railroad in the 1830s.[81] In August 1835, after working the Waltersville quarry, Putney and Riddle signed a twenty-year lease to the quarry lands from Alexander Walters. The Waltersville Quarry was their flagship enterprise, located on the Baltimore County side of the Patapsco. They built the two-mile-long Waltersville Rail Road (a.k.a. Putney and Riddle Railroad) from the quarry on the other side of the Patapsco crossing a bridge to the mainline. This allowed them to efficiently transport their products to market.[82]

Perhaps due to the anticipation of the planned Washington Branch railroad connecting to the Guilford quarries much like the mainline connected to the Waltersville quarry, Putney and Riddle had also obtained 170 acres of land from John Warfield for the start of the Guilford quarries

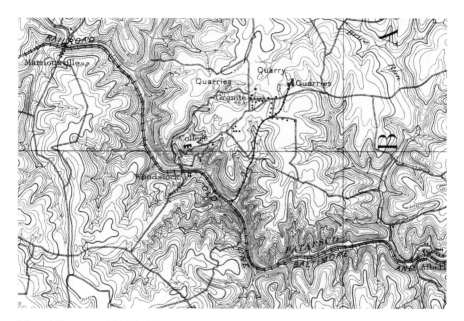

Map of Putney and Riddle Bridge location, 1892. *USGS Topo Map.*

on February 4, 1835. Their interest in the Guilford area was based on a possible rail line being built from the B&O Washington Branch to the quarries, and Riddle even recommended buying stock for the Savage Railroad, which he had planned to extend to the quarries.[83] However, the Savage Railroad did not link farther than to the Savage Mills, and a rail line was not built to the quarries until 1901.

Putney and Riddle accumulated a great deal of debt starting their granite quarry business, and after just a few busy years, they were forced to sell. Granite sills were being replaced by wooden stringers, or ties, and the railroads were not going to be a steady source of income for granite quarries anymore. In 1839, Putney and Riddle agreed to meet their creditor obligations by selling their holdings and business equipment through a court-appointed trustee named Edward Green. They owned a great deal of property at Waltersville, including a railroad, a road next to the B&O, rough stone, tools and rigging connected with the quarry, household and office furniture, horses, oxen, grain and the stone rigging and lumber at the yard used in Baltimore.[84]

After Riddle and Putney's properties were liquidated to pay their debts, Edward Green acquired the Waltersville quarry with his business partner Joshua Sumwalt. Edward Green, trustee, sold the Guilford quarry lands to

Reuben Aler, who in turn sold them to the stoneworkers John B. Emery and Cyrus Gault in January 1845[85] Emery and Gault were also involved with a quarry at Woodstock, and Cyrus Gault's grandson would be part owner of quarries at Guilford many decades later.

The next year, Emery and Gault sold all but eight acres of the property to Jesse and James DuVall, who then sold the land to Amon Lowry and Robert Isherwood just a month later.[86] Unfortunately, it is easier to find that they sold the land than what they did with it, and how it changed.

INTO THE WASHINGTON MONUMENT

This exhaustive list of owners is meant to bring your attention to Cyrus Gault and Amon Lowry. In 1851, the City Council of Baltimore resolved that a stone should be prepared for the Washington National Monument in D.C., as Baltimore's contribution. The contract to provide such a stone was given to Cyrus Gault and his brother Matthew, and in 1853, it was announced that Baltimore's contribution to the Washington Monument would be a block of

Image of the finished block of Guilford granite inside the D.C. Washington Monument. *National Park Service.*

stone cut from the quarry owned by Amon Lowry. William F. Atkinson was charged with forming this block into a work of art.[87] This most famous and unusual block of granite from the Guilford quarries made its way into the Washington Monument.

The inscription on the block of stone placed at the 140-foot level in the interior of the monument reads:

> *Anno 1850. By the citizens of Baltimore. May Heaven to this Union continue its beneficence. May brotherly affection with Union be perpetual. May the Free Constitution, which is the work of our ancestors, be sacredly maintained, and its administration be stamped with wisdom and virtue.*[88]

The Baltimore stone was one of more than 190 memorial stones inside the Washington Monument representing states, cities, groups and individuals during the first phase of its construction.

Over a fifty-eight-year period (1853–1911) Guilford granite was reported in newspapers as being used for at least the following structures:[89]

- Baltimore Custom House
- U.S. Capitol
- U.S. Treasury Building
- General/Senator Philip Reed memorial
- Lieutenant Colonel William Watson memorial monument
- Mount St. Mary's Church cornerstone
- Mexican Veterans Monument
- Gettysburg monument of soldiers from Hanover
- Hyattsville First Presbyterian Church Chapel
- Lutheran Church in Ohio

GUILFORD AND WALTERSVILLE GRANITE COMPANY

Perhaps Putney and Riddle started a trend by being the first to own both the Waltersville and Guilford quarries in the 1830s, even if it was only for a few years. After Putney and Riddle, the Waltersville quarry was operated by Edward Green and Joshua Sumwalt until about 1865, when Atwood Blunt and his wife took over. The Guilford and Waltersville story starts around 1872, when the Blunts leased their land to Ansley Gill and James McMahon.

Image of the Guilford and Waltersville Quarry in Granite, Maryland. *USGS.*

Gill and McMahon ran the quarry, in what became the town of Granite, until McMahon's death around 1887, when the firm of Gill and McMahon was dissolved. By 1888, Gill had joined with William H. Johnson and, presumably with the knowledge of the granite quarries in Guilford, formed the joint stock company called the Guilford and Waltersville Granite Company. As part of this company, they were joined by George Mann, Hugh Hanna and Messrs. Grey and Sons from Philadelphia and Peter Hamilton of Baltimore. Hamilton gifted the Druid Hill Park sundial to the City of Baltimore in 1890.[90]

A fifteen-year lease agreement with Henry A. Penny, Ansley Gill and William H. Johnson in 1888 provided the Guilford and Waltersville Granite Company with land for "the purpose of quarrying, cutting, hauling and removing said granite and for dumping," as well as "the privilege…to construct a railroad." There had been plans for a railroad to connect with the Washington Branch line since 1835, and this was the closest anyone had come to making that happen. With the opening of the Patuxent Branch line at Savage connected to the Washington Branch main line, expectations seemed high that a further extension to Guilford would follow. The lease from Henry A. Penny specifically mentioned a possible railroad.[91]

The USGS conducted a site visit to Guilford in 1908 to examine the quarries. Although "work had been suspended some time prior" to the visit, it identified the Guilford and Waltersville Granite Company quarry downstream of the large Maryland Granite Company quarry (beyond the bend of the river) on the east side of the river.[92] This location is verified by a deed from the company to John Sieling in 1912, who in 1923 sold the land to Louis Perna, who was identified on tax records as owning the land on the east side of the river where an abandoned quarry is currently located, owned by HoCo.[93] You can see the quarry filled with water even today.

On September 17, 1921, the State of Maryland declared the charter of the Guilford and Waltersville Granite Company null and void for failure to pay the franchise tax. In February 1924, Oliver C. Putney sued the company to be allowed to remove his machinery from the land leased from the company.[94] Perhaps this action was responsible for the company charter being revived in June the same year after lapsing for nonpayment of taxes. In April 1925, receivers were appointed for the company, indicating it was being dissolved.

Chapter 4

COTTON MILLS

In 1808, the Ellicotts sold much of their original land purchased along the Patapsco River in Baltimore County to the Union Manufacturing Company. By 1810, Union had begun operating as the first cotton mill in Maryland, only twenty years after the first cotton mill was established in the United States.[95] In the area that became HoCo, the first cotton mill was the Eagle Mill on the Patapsco listed in the 1820 census.[96] The second was in Savage, chartered in 1821, followed by land purchases the next two years for the mill site and operations. By 1825, Savage Mill was running one thousand spindles and 120 power looms employing two hundred people.[97] Cotton mills were originally powered by the same method as gristmills, water descending along the fall line, before converting to steam in the latter half of the 1800s.

The next HoCo cotton mill was the Elysville Mill, chartered in 1828, followed by Okisko, Alberton and finally Daniels. The rains and flooding of Hurricane Agnes destroyed the Daniels Mill in 1972. By 1834, a cotton mill was part of the Guilford Factory that was later owned by James S. Gary and Son. The son, James A. Gary, became postmaster general of the United States under President McKinley and ran the Alberton, Laurel and Guilford Mills in the late 1800s. He also built two memorial Methodist churches, one in Guilford in 1872, named after his firstborn daughter, Alberta Georgette Gary, who died of scarlet fever at five years old. The other church was built in Alberton in 1879 in memory of his father, James Sullivan Gary.[98]

When Guilford Factory was put up for sale in the 1840s, William H. Baldwin and George Wheeler agreed to the purchase. When the title

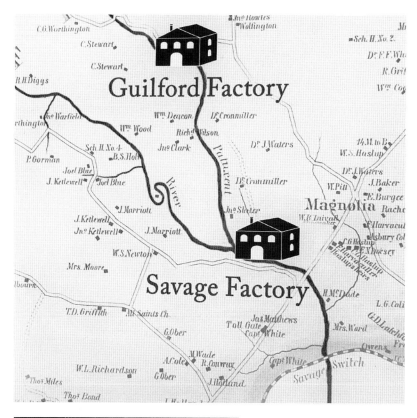

Above: Map of Guilford and Savage Factories. *Robinson Nature Center.*

Left: Portrait of Alberta Georgette Gary, circa 1863. *Courtesy of the University of Virginia, Albert and Shirley Small Special Collections Library.*

came into question, Baldwin and Wheeler backed out of the sale. Baldwin later bought the Savage Manufacturing Company in 1859, expanded and improved it to make it one of the largest cotton factories in the East. We wonder what the fate of the Guilford Factory would have been if Baldwin had purchased it as well.

Joshua Barney, the Guilford Pirate

Commodore Joshua Barney (July 6, 1759–December 10, 1818) is well known for being a privateer (legal pirate) for the U.S. government during the start of the War of 1812 and for his heroic defense of Washington, D.C., but ultimate defeat during the Battle of Bladensburg in 1814, where he was mortally wounded. Outnumbered and outmatched by the British at Bladensburg, Barney engaged and slowed the enemy but could not stop them from their march to D.C., where they burned the Capitol building.[99] Barney was known for many things, but he wasn't known for his interest in mill lands in the Guilford area and his influence on the founding of the Savage Manufacturing Company (SMC).

Few realize Barney lived among the early residents of Guilford and Savage between 1811 and 1818. After the death of his first wife in 1808, he married Harriet Coale of Guilford in the spring of 1809. Harriet's mother was Sarah Ridgely, whose family had owned their plantation, including a mill, along the east side of the Little Patuxent River for many years. Harriett and her mother, Sarah, were descendants of Henry Ridgely, who had patented these lands in the late 1600s. Before moving into his new home, Barney himself patented river land just downstream of the future location of Guilford Mill in 1809. Called "The First Attempt," that land was described as "vacant" and not claimed by other patents or deeds.[100]

In 1811, Barney patented "Mill Race," claiming vacant land adjoining the lands called White's Contrivance, Warfield's Range and Mill Land, where the ruins of the Savage Mill Dam are located today. He also purchased "Harry's Lott" for his wife and her family and, when the land was resurveyed, claimed additional lands. Also in 1811, he resurveyed an adjoining land called Cole's Choice, claiming additional vacant lands, and in 1814 did a resurvey of another nearby land patent called "Cocksell."

What all these lands had in common was the Little Patuxent River. Barney basically claimed the banks of the river between what is now near Lake Elkhorn downstream to Savage, with the exception of the Guilford

Mill area and the Mill Seat in Partnership adjacent to Harry's Lott. The land resurveys often resulted from legal challenges based on improved surveying methods or claiming of vacant lands. The usual result was increasing the land acreage of the plaintiff. The resurvey of Harry's Lott was done with his wife, Harriett, and her brother Alfred and sister Anne as co-beneficiaries.

Due to Barney's service to his country, he had little time to manage his own landholdings. But in 1809, his daughter Caroline, from his first marriage, married an effective attorney, Nathaniel Williams, who handled those matters. Williams represented Barney in the purchase of Harry's Lott in 1811 and in its April 1818 sale. Williams was also one of the four brothers who would create SMC in 1821.[101]

After Barney was wounded in the 1814 Battle of Bladensburg, he returned to Guilford and retained a naval commission. His desire was to finally relocate to Elizabethtown in Hardin County, Kentucky, where he had purchased over fifty thousand acres of land. Although Barney, his wife and his sister-in-law Anne had visited some of their Kentucky holdings traveling by horseback, it was not feasible to do so with the entire family and their belongings, including their many servants and household furnishings.

They left Guilford in October 1818 and headed toward Brownsville, Pennsylvania, where they would take a boat down the Monongahela River into the Ohio River at Pittsburgh and then follow that downstream to Kentucky. Due to low flows in the river, the journey was difficult, and Barney provided some physical assistance along with others on the various maneuvers. The physical nature of the trip was too much for him and he made it only to Pittsburgh. On December 1, 1818, at age fifty-nine, he died from complications of his wound from four years earlier.[102]

While this is never truly mentioned in any town history, we believe Barney influenced the building of Savage Mill. He knew of the demand for making sailcloth. His second wife's family owned Harry's Lott adjacent to White's Contrivance and the mill, he received a land patent for a millrace just upstream of White's Mill and he had a relationship with the Williams brothers. In his privateering days, he likely knew Michael McBlair and John Hollins, who submitted the incorporation papers for SMC in December 1821. Joshua Barney deserves credit for influencing the creation of Savage Mill.[103]

JOHN SAVAGE AND THE WILLIAMS BROTHERS

When the Williams brothers were starting their new cotton mill on the Little Patuxent River in the early 1820s, they named it in honor of John Savage, a wealthy Philadelphian who had loaned them $20,000 for their venture. There has been some confusion about who this John Savage was, with some incorrectly identifying him as the son of a wealthy plantation-owning family who was born in Jamaica in 1790 and died in 1834, the same year as our John Savage. This story benefits from research assistance by Gerald Ueckermann and will attempt to set the record straight.

John Savage was the son of Darby and Ann (Molley) Savage, who were wed in 1762.[104] He was born in Philadelphia on May 30, 1766, and baptized on June 1, 1766, at St. Joseph's Catholic Church.[105] Darby bought property in 1770 on Chestnut Street in Philadelphia and was still living there in 1791, with his occupation listed as "gentleman."[106] In 1787, Darby Savage had pew no. 15 registered at the St. Mary's Church in Philadelphia; it remained so until his death in 1780.[107] By 1789, Darby's son John had taken over pew no. 15.[108]

John Savage was a Philadelphia shipping merchant who, by the mid-1780s, was doing business in the Caribbean, including Antigua.[109] The first advertisement for his business partnership with Joseph Dugan, called Savage & Dugan, appeared in 1799 to sell or charter the "Ship Hope."[110] On the 1800 census, John Savage was listed as a merchant living in the Philadelphia Dock Ward.[111] After many profitable years, Savage and Dugan dissolved their business partnership in 1821.[112] John Savage died on November 18, 1834, in Philadelphia. His will named a "natural" son,

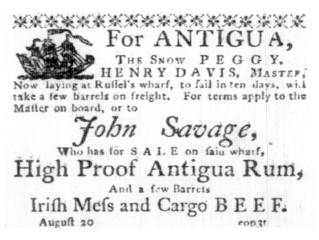

Advertisement for Antigua Run supplied by John Savage. *From the* American Daily Advertiser.

John Savage Jr., and a natural daughter, Margaret Savage, but he does not appear to have ever married. He also named Margaret Savage's mother, Elizabeth Crosby, in his will.[113]

John Savage and George Williams were both merchants involved in shipping, John in Philadelphia and George in Baltimore.[114] They interacted with each other during their role as directors of the Bank of the United States in 1817 and 1818.[115] It was probably a natural connection, as the two men had common business interests with investments in shipping, and the concept of manufacturing sailcloth made sense for each of them. Along with Joshua Barney, they found a site along the Little Patuxent River in HoCo to establish one of the longest-operating cotton mills on the East Coast.[116]

George, Amos, Cumberland and Nathaniel were the four Williams brothers who founded SMC with the help of John Savage. John invested $20,000 in George Williams's new mill business and held some lands in collateral, per a March 4, 1823 indenture between SMC and John Savage.[117] It seemed that John Savage was interested in the cotton-milling business, as he also lent $3,000 the following year to Edward Gray, who owned the Patapsco Cotton Mill.[118] These are the only two area mills we have found in which John Savage made investments. There is no record that John Savage ever visited the town that the Williams brothers named for him.

After Savage died in 1834, his heirs eventually filed suit to recover the $20,000 debt owed to them. The 1854 Chancery Court records show that the Williams brothers were always aware of the debt to Savage but never had the funds to pay it. The lawsuit by the Savage heirs, and others, is what led to the Williams's eventual sale of the mill in 1859.[119]

Only one image of John Savage could be found: a portrait painted by the artist Thomas Sully around 1824, in the National Portrait Gallery of the Smithsonian.[120] In a 1922 *Catalogue of the Memorial Exhibition of Portraits by Thomas Sully* published by the Pennsylvania Academy of the Fine Arts, incorrect biographical information was included for the John Savage portrait, identifying him as the John Savage born in Jamaica in 1790. But the portrait was loaned by

Portrait of John Savage (1765–1834), namesake of the Savage Manufacturing Company. *Wikimedia.*

"a great-grandson, D. Fitzhugh Savage" of Philadelphia. Fortunately, we can confirm through census and death records that Daniel Fitzhugh Savage was indeed the great-grandson of our John Savage, born in 1866, and of the firm Savage and Dugan. D. Fitzhugh's parents were John Savage Jr. and Isabella Swift Fitzhugh Savage.[121] John Savage Jr.'s parents were John and Adelaide, and John's father was our John Savage.[122]

Becoming Guilford Factory

Developing mill areas earned the name of factory when more than one type of mill was present. Guilford Mills had long been composed of a sawmill and gristmill, and in December 1817 it was described in the *Baltimore Patriot* as being a 130-acre merchant mill and sawmill and "a good dwelling house, store house, cooper's shop, stabling…a young apple orchard of about 200 trees…and four or five hundred flour barrels."

James Owings took over the mill in 1830, and in 1832, it was referred to as the Guilford Factory. By 1834, a cotton mill was added, producing cotton yarn and cotton chain. In 1836, Owings advertised it as Guilford Cotton Factory and soon began looking for cotton spinners. William Baldwin and George Wheeler agreed to purchase Guilford Cotton Factory in 1845, but James Owings was not able to provide a clean title because his former partner, Isaac Paul, never deeded his interest in the property to Owings. Over the next few years, there were different legal actions regarding the ownership of the Guilford Cotton Factory, including Owings's unsuccessful lawsuit against Baldwin and Wheeler in 1849 to go through with their agreed purchase. Afterward, it was owned by Henry H. Owings, the brother of James. By this time, Baldwin and Wheeler had shifted their sights to the Savage Manufacturing Company, which they purchased in 1859.[123]

In the 1850 census of manufacturers for the Howard District of Anne Arundel County, businesses reported near the Guilford Factory included the granite quarry owned by Amon Lowry and a gristmill and a sawmill operated by Henry H. Owings. In the Howard District mortality census for that year, a note was provided that stated, "There are two cotton factories that have not been in operation since '45 but they are small, not running many looms or spindles: one is situated at Elysville and the other at Guilford."[124]

Stephen P. Heath Sr. bought the Guilford Cotton Factory from Henry H. Owings in 1867 and mortgaged the property to cotton mill owner James S. Gary. Gary died in 1870, and Heath died in 1874, leaving their children to

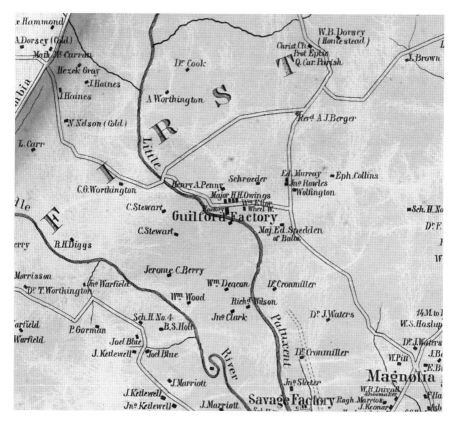

Martenet's 1860 map of the Guilford Factory area. *Library of Congress.*

work out the mortgage debt. In 1875, the Guilford Factory was sold at public auction, and James A. Gary purchased it. An experienced Stephen Heath Jr. would continue as the proprietor of the mill.

By 1878, the cotton factory was producing nineteen thousand pounds of cotton each month. A newspaper article on Guilford reported that "the character of cloth made at this factory is a heavy, unbleached muslin, which is termed Alabama and Palmetto; No. 1, heavy Osnaburgs running about three yards to the pound."[125] It was also stated that this was the most successful and profitable of Gary's mills. The mill operated smoothly, and in 1881, it was reported to have 1,200 spindles and 50 looms making Osnaburgs.[126]

In 1882, it was reported that the mill had a "stone dam 200 feet long and 8 feet high, a race 2,500 feet long, and a utilized fall of 14 feet." However, on March 20, 1888, the *Baltimore Sun* reported that the Guilford Factory dam had washed away in a storm, making the mill dependent on steam power.

The ruins of the dam are still visible. The *Sun* reported on August 14 and 16, 1890, that the cotton mill had burned down and seventy men had lost their jobs. Gary offered the workers employment at his mills in Alberton on the Patapsco (most recently called Daniels), and Stephen P. Heath Jr. became proprietor of a new mill in Baltimore built by Gary.

In 1894, Gary sold the mill property to August Brunner, who in turn sold it within five years to the quarries, ending the story of the Guilford Factory. This is the same August Brunner who became the postmaster for Guilford starting on August 29, 1888.[127]

Chapter 5

The Baltimore and Ohio Railroad

Baltimore City is home to the internationally renowned B&O Railroad Museum, and the first passenger railroad in America was established there. The line opened for travel from Baltimore to Ellicott's Mills in May 1830 and led to the development of the area that would become Ellicott City. Just thirteen miles by track to Baltimore, along the Patapsco River, sits the Ellicott City train station, which has survived longer than any other railroad station or terminal in the United States. Opened sometime in the spring of 1831, the building represented the first major stop on the Old Main Line on its eventual way to Wheeling, Virginia, on the Ohio River.[128]

There is much hidden history to share about the B&O, but we focus this chapter on the branch railroad of the B&O that brought life to the Guilford and Savage area over its iconic bridges.

The early B&O Railroad started to build sills and stringers, stabilize track beds and build bridge abutments by using HoCo granite to create the first large-scale commercial granite uses in the county. As noted previously, the Woodstock granite quarries were prominently used in the early 1830s to support the B&O, and the same promise was held for the Guilford granite quarries as they opened in 1834.

The Patuxent Branch Rail Line

The history of the Patuxent Branch Rail (PBR) Line began in 1835 when the main Washington Branch Line opened, linking Baltimore to Washington,

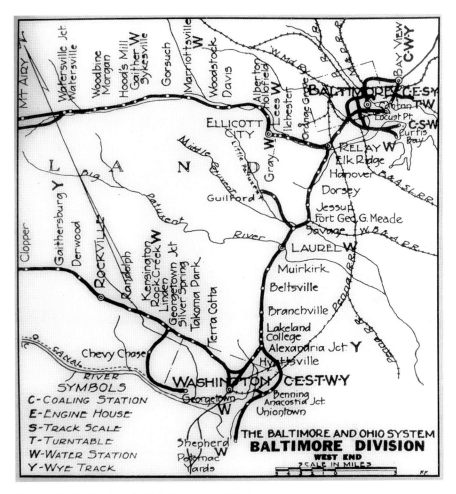

Map of the B&O railroad. *HoCo Recreation and Parks.*

D.C. As the Washington Branch opened, there was hope that the line would be extended to Guilford, as noted in the October 13, 1835 issue of the *American and Commercial Daily Advertiser.* It stated that "nineteen miles from Baltimore, the Savage Railroad diverges from the Washington branch, and leads to the Savage Factory and the most valuable quarries of granite in the neighborhood," referring to the quarries at Guilford.

The Savage Rail Road Company was formed in 1835 to connect the Washington Branch Line to the Savage Factory and Guilford Quarries and, from there, directly to Baltimore and D.C. The company's charter was published in the September 22, 1835 *Baltimore Gazette and Daily Advertiser,*

MARYLAND DISTRICT
BALTIMORE DIVISION—WEST

Index Reference	SIDING CAPACITY Cars 42 feet long					Telegraph Call	Station Number	STATIONS AND SIDINGS with character references, population (census of 1920), and additional index references	County	Miles from	Savage	AGENTS, Etc.
	Passing	Company	Joint	Private	Loading or Unloading Capacity							
								Patuxent Branch				
1260							C 10	Savage (1224) .... Md.		116.9	0.0	
C1260				5			C101B	J. K. L. Ross .... "		117.9	1.0	
1261		26			14		C101	Savage Factory .... "		118.0	1.1	
1262		17			10		C101A	Gabbro .... "		118.8	1.9	
1263		14					C103A	B. F. Pope Siding .... "		119.8	2.9	Dallas E. Waters .... F.
1264		15			15		C104C	Maryland Granite Co .... "		121.2	4.3	
1265							C104	Guilford, P. 50—W .... "		121.2	4.3	
1266		25			25		C104E	Howard Granite Co .... "		121.2	4.3	

Patuxent Branch Line station list, 1922. *Courtesy of B&O Railroad Historical Society.*

and it was clear that its intent was "construction and repair of a Rail-Road from the lateral branch of the Baltimore and Ohio Rail-Road, to the city of Washington, and connected therewith; commencing near to the point where said lateral branch crosses the little Patuxent, and extending up said little Patuxent, passing by the Savage Factory, for a distance of not more than six miles." The length of the Patuxent Branch ended up being about 4.1 miles when it was completed in 1901.[129]

The Savage Rail Road Company operated using horsepower and never ended up extending beyond Savage Factory itself. Amos Williams, of the four Williams brothers and the company agent at the factory, was one of the primary forces for this company, and many of the stockholders were not pleased with this investment or the 10 percent annual fee for the cost of the railroad that Williams wanted to charge the SMC. This was contrasted with the highest railroad dividend in the country of 6 percent being charged by the Providence Rail Road. George Williams wrote in a deposition that "Amos A. Williams had his own way out there. That was the way the use of the Road was forced on the Company."[130] Even brothers were against each other legally.

A bridge costing $2,000 to $3,000 was constructed to Savage Factory, crossing the Little Patuxent River, but the railroad company only lasted until about July 1844.[131] We don't know the fate of the original bridge, but in 1985, archaeologists believed they may have found it buried beneath the river where the existing Bollman Bridge stands.[132] More research is needed to determine whether other rail bridges were attempted to reconnect Savage Factory to the mainline.

In 1887, a B&O Patuxent Branch Rail (PBR) spur was finally built to Savage Factory across the newly installed Bollman Bridge with, again, the hope of connecting to the Guilford Quarries.[133] While the quarries' commercial business increased, it was initially held back by the lack of easy transportation to the rail lines by horse. Quarry blocks could now be hauled over the macadamized roads to the Savage Mill station, saving more than a mile of effort. In 1889, the B&O Railroad issued a book on its stations in which the PBR was officially listed at a distance of 1.3 miles.[134]

Maryland Granite Company took over the large quarry in 1901 and completed the rail line between Guilford and Savage Mill, providing us with the Guilford Quarry Pratt Through Truss Bridge that lies near Guilford Road today. The full PBR line of the B&O Railroad operated between 1902 and 1928 and contained several commercial stops between the main Washington Branch Line at Savage Switch and the end of the PBR at the Guilford Quarries.[135]

In 1928, 2.5 miles of the PBR between Guilford to Savage Mill was officially closed. The declaration of abandonment by the B&O stated that there was no industry along the tributary and the quarries had been abandoned in 1924, with only fifteen train carloads of crushed stone sent along the line that year. This, in contrast to the hundreds of carloads in earlier years, shows the quarries' decline in production. We do not know which quarry was still crushing stone at the time.[136] Today, the Patuxent Branch and Wincopin Green Trails occupy the path that the B&O Railroad traveled over 115 years ago.[137]

THE FIRST AND LAST BOLLMAN BRIDGES

The last known example of a Bollman truss bridge resides in Savage, crossing the Little Patuxent River between Savage Mill and what used to be the PBR line of the B&O Railroad. The design was created by Wendel Bollman, a civil engineer and master of road for the B&O Railroad Company in the 1840s. This bridge was designated the first national Historic Civil Engineering Landmark in 1966 by the American Society of Civil Engineers and, in 1972, recognized in the National Register of Historic Places.[138] The nearby Bollman Bridge Elementary School was named for the famous bridge and its designer.

Surprisingly, there was an earlier bridge designed by Wendel Bollman near this location installed in 1850. This 1850 Bollman bridge replaced the original wooden bridge crossing the Little Patuxent River on the Washington Branch Line that was lost to flooding in 1847. This was the prototype bridge designed by Bollman, the first iron bridge ever used by the B&O Railroad.

WENDEL BOLLMAN.   J. H. TEGMEYER.   JAMES CLARK.

BOLLMAN'S
PATENT
Iron Railroad Bridge.

The undersigned are prepared to execute orders for Bollman's Patent Iron Railroad Bridge, and to furnish Drawings, Estimates, &c., &c., for

BRIDGES, ROOFS, ENGINE HOUSES, MACHINE SHOPS, &c.

Or to contract for the erection of the same, in any part of the United States or abroad, with promptness and upon satisfactory terms.

Address

W. BOLLMAN & CO., Baltimore, Md.

Among other references, may be named the following gentlemen:—

WM. PARKER, ESQ., *Civil Engineer, Boston.*
WM. J. MCALPINE, ESQ., *Civil Engineer, Albany, N. Y.*
ISAAC R. TRIMBLE, ESQ., *Civil Engineer, Baltimore.*
CAPT. M. C. MEIGS, *U. S. Engineer Corps, Washington.*
COL. CROZET, *Civil Engineer, Washington.*
HERMAN HAUPT, ESQ., *Civil Engineer, Philadelphia.*

Bollmann's Iron Suspension and Trussed Bridge.—
On the second floor is to be seen the delicate model of
a bridge, which from its appearance would be thought
scarcely able to sustain any weight. It represents a
space of 75 feet in the clear between abutments, the
depth and width of the truss being ten feet, and is built
on a scale of an inch to the foot, or one-twelfth of its
proper dimensions. It is certainly new in principle, and
exhibits the precise pattern of the superstructure of the
viaduct over the Little Patuxent river, near the Savage
Factory, on the Washington Branch Railroad, 16 miles
from Baltimore. This viaduct, together with that over
the Eastern branch at Bladensburgh, was carried away
by the destructive flood of 7th Oct., 1847. Both were
originally stone arches of 50 feet span, and are replaced
by plain stone abutments connected by iron trusses, upon the plan of the present model. The one over the
Patuxent is recently completed, and the other will be
finished by spring. By the use of this iron truss, instead of a stone arch, a large saving of expense in construction has been made, and an equally strong, safe
and durable structure obtained; while the water way
has been increased 50 per cent.

Opposite: Bollman Bridge advertisement, from *The Book of the Great Railway Celebrations of 1857*.

Left: The first iron suspension and trussed bridge by Bollman, 1850. *From the* Baltimore Sun.

It was tested over the Little Patuxent River at the Savage Switch station on the Washington Branch Line, just a mile downstream from the current location.[139] It proved the design was satisfactory before the patent was awarded in 1852.[140]

We were confused about the location of the original bridge for quite some time because many of the descriptions of it claimed that it was at Savage Factory, or at least at Savage Station. One of our early professional lessons learned was not to be afraid of contacting the experts. In this case, there was no greater expert than Robert Vogel, formerly curator of mechanical and civil engineering at the Smithsonian Institution Museum of American History for thirty-one years. The accolades for this man include the founding of the Society for Industrial Archaeology, in part based on his work on the Bollman Bridge, which became a Historic Civil Engineering Landmark supported by his research and outreach efforts.

Vogel wrote *The Engineering Contributions of Wendel Bollman* in 1966, so we couldn't find a better person to contact.[141] During a phone conversation in February 2019, Vogel was emphatic that the original Bollman bridge was on the Washington Branch rail line going across the Little Patuxent River near, but not at, Savage Factory. The name Savage Factory was also sometimes used for the railroad station at Savage Switch.[142]

The bridge currently standing at Savage Mill was constructed in 1869 and occupied a location somewhere else on the B&O system, often claimed to be on the main line. There were other Bollman truss bridges used on the B&O in HoCo, including at Elysville where James A. Gary had a cotton mill, Marriottsville, Ilchester and Laurel over the Patuxent River.[143] We wonder if any of these older bridges could have been the one placed at Savage Mill. It was moved to its current location in 1887, when the B&O formally opened the Patuxent Branch line connecting the main Washington Branch line with Savage Factory in January 1888. However, information found in a *Baltimore Sun* article from December 20, 1881, seems to change the date of constructing this Bollman Bridge to 1881. It reports that "Mr. W.H. Baldwin, owner of the property, recently completed a new truss-bridge over the Patuxent. Between the mill and the Washington Branch of the Baltimore and Ohio Railroad, 186 by 19 feet, and 26 feet above the water-level." Those dimensions closely fit the current Bollman bridge at Savage Mill.

The Bollman, and Pratt, truss bridge designs for the B&O allowed the bridges to be portable. Once they were no longer structurally sufficient for current use, either because of the road changing or engines in that area becoming too heavy, they were often disassembled and moved to other locations. The PBR Line did not require as rugged a bridge, due to lighter rails and engines. The current Bollman bridge and the PBR Line to Savage Mill were likely in routine operation until the mill closed in 1947. It is worth seeing, if you haven't.

BETWEEN THE PRATT BRIDGES

A unique area exists along the PBR Line between the two bridges designed by Caleb Pratt and his son. Of the four bridges on the old PBR Line that opened in 1902, two of them were Pratt bridges—one crossing the Little Patuxent River at Guilford and the other downstream crossing the Middle Patuxent River at Savage. These bridges were moved to their current locations from where they had previously been two spans of bridge no. 10 of the B&O district 2, middle division—likely in Ohio, where the only "middle division" was found and where many of those bridges eventually made their way out of state. [144]

These Pratt bridges are named for Caleb and his son Thomas Willis Pratt, both of New England, who patented their design in 1844 (patent no. 3,523, Pratt 1844). Their design used wood for the upright compression members and wrought iron for the diagonal tension members, which was the opposite of the predecessor Howe truss bridge. However, with the success of the all-metal Bollman bridges, the Pratt truss bridges were eventually made of all wrought iron and became increasingly popular due to their simplicity of design and ease of construction in the field. [145]

Guilford Quarry Pratt Through Truss Bridge, circa 1920s. *Smithsonian Institution.*

Gabbro Bridge, circa 1920s. *Smithsonian Institution.*

The lower bridge just upstream of Savage was called the Gabbro Bridge, but not because it was made of the hard traprock called gabbro that is still being quarried at the nearby Savage Stone quarry. It was known as the Gabbro Bridge because of its proximity to the Gabbro rail station on the PBR line that served the W.T. Manning quarries. The bridge comprised two parts: the 93-foot-long iron bridge and a 148-foot timber trestle. The bridge and trestle are long gone, but the granite abutments are still there—one intact, providing a scenic view, and the other toppled into the river.

The bridge abutments were made of Guilford granite but had to be encased in concrete since they would be mostly submerged by the pond above Savage Dam. The pond was only a few feet below the bridge, as you can see from the photo. The 1918 Interstate Commerce Commission valuation documents indicate that the timber trestle for this bridge was originally connected to the Pratt bridge serving the Guilford quarries before it was moved here.

Along the Patuxent Branch Trail, which was built by HoCo in the early 2000s, between these bridges are a number of historic sites, some of which have visible ruins. Just upstream of the Gabbro Bridge is one of the gabbro quarries that was somewhat elongated along a ridge, likely using a small-gauge rail to transport the stone from the quarries to the stone crusher. Nearby, ruins of a large stone crusher cluster around the landscape.

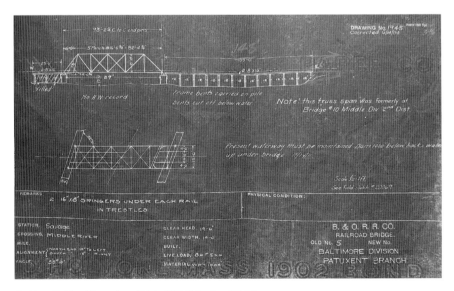

Gabbro Bridge blueprint, 1904. *ICC Valuation, NARA.*

A little farther upstream from this stone crusher are the ruins of a crib dam. Crib dams were among the earliest type of dam and looked like narrow log cabins filled with dirt. They were often anchored on the sides by stones. You can still see the crib dam stones and earth standing about ten feet high where the Wincopin Green trail descends on the west side of the Little Patuxent River. On a sign at the Wincopin trailhead, HoCo Rec and Parks wrote that it believes the bridge was built between 1802 and 1804 for the Savage Mills.[146]

About 1835, the Savage Manufacturing Company was expanding to include an iron furnace that would require additional waterpower. One of the sources was on the Little Patuxent River, often referred to as the North Branch of the Patuxent during the 1800s, diverting water in a race via a dam, and it quite possibly could have been this crib dam. In 1847, the *Baltimore Sun* reported that "at the Savage factory, one of the dams gave way, and great loss was sustained—the main dam was only saved by the water rushing through the race, and making a track for itself." Could it be that the *Sun* was referring to the crib dam being destroyed?[147]

W.T. Manning stone crusher, circa 1920s. *Smithsonian Institution.*

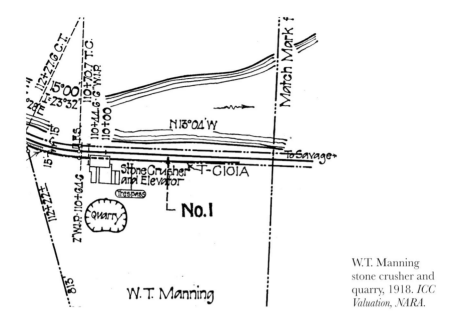

W.T. Manning stone crusher and quarry, 1918. *ICC Valuation, NARA.*

Upstream of the crib dam was the large B.F. Pope gabbro quarry with the ruins of a stone crusher. The Gabbro Bridge, W.T. Manning quarry and stone crusher, the crib dam and the B.F. Pope quarry and stone crusher are all located along the Wincopin Green Trail on what used to be the Patuxent Branch line. Farther upstream is the location for Hammond's lost mill—gone, without a trace to be found. On a ridge to the east is Commodore Joshua Barney's house and finally, a little farther upstream, we come to the Guilford quarries and the other Pratt Bridge.

The "sister" bridge to the Gabbro Bridge is the one farthest upstream, called the Guilford Quarry Pratt Through Truss Bridge, which was officially listed in the National Park Service's National Register of Historic Places (SG100006648) on June 2, 2021. This bridge was constructed at this site in either late 1901 or early 1902 to complete the extension of the B&O PBR line to Guilford, which opened to freight in April 1902. Because of the relationship of the bridge to the Maryland Granite Company, it is also sometimes called the Willis J. Carter bridge.

Chapter 6

Seeking Freedom

B y the 1830s, states south of the Mason-Dixon Line, like Maryland, were
supporting slavery, and HoCo was no exception. In 1860, 21.5 percent
of the population of HoCo (2,862 out of a total population of 13,338)
was enslaved, about double of the number of free Blacks.[148] The topic of
Maryland and HoCo slavery is entrenched in our government from the
beginning of the founding of Maryland.

During the 1860 presidential election in HoCo, only one person voted for
Abraham Lincoln and the dissolution of slavery. The voting population was
split between two candidates supporting enslavement, but their views about
remaining in the Union differed. A moderate supporting the constitution
and maintaining the Union, John Bell, received 54 percent of the vote.
Proslavery and anti-Union John Breckingridge received 34 percent, and
Stephen Douglas, with a states' rights view on slavery, received 12 percent.[149]

The four Maryland governors claiming HoCo as their home, Thomas
Watkins Ligon, John Lee Carroll, George Howard and Edwin Warfield,
were all associated with slavery and racism. Unfortunately, four of the
county's main government buildings are named for these men. HoCo at
times seemed more like the Deep South than part of a border state. In
1922, Maryland Historical Society member Edward Breckinridge Lowndes
characterized HoCo as follows:

> *The people generally are somewhat unlike their neighbors in Carroll,
> Montgomery and Baltimore counties, for they are more Southern in their*

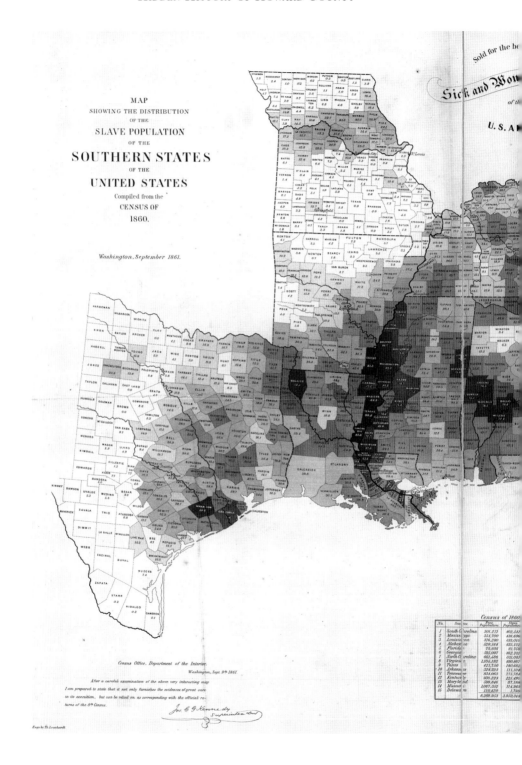

MAP
SHOWING THE DISTRIBUTION
OF THE
SLAVE POPULATION
OF THE
SOUTHERN STATES
OF THE
UNITED STATES
Compiled from the
CENSUS OF
1860.

Washington, September 1861.

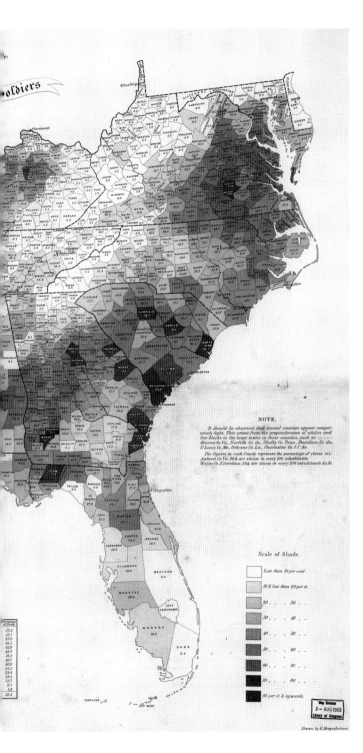

Census map of slave population, 1860. *U.S. Census Bureau.*

THE PRESIDENTIAL ELECTION.

VIRGINIA.

The Richmond Whig, received last night, says Clay county has given Bell 84, and Webster gives him 13 majority. Bell, therefore, has carried the State by 250 plurality. It does not think the official vote will reduce the plurality of Bell.

The Enquirer puts Bell 396 ahead, and says Webster is still to be heard from. The Dispatch makes Bell's plurality 254 without Webster.

Official Vote of Maryland.

The following is the official vote of Maryland at the recent election, compiled from the original returns on file in the executive department:

Counties.	Breckinridge.	Bell.	Douglas.	Lin.
Allegany	979	1521	1203	522
Anne Arundel	1017	1041	98	3
Baltimore city	14,956	12,604	1503	1083
Baltimore county	3305	3388	449	37
Caroline	616	712	100	12
Carroll	1791	2295	339	59
Calvert	386	399	43	1
Cecil	1506	1792	393	158
Charles	723	430	38	6
Dorchester	1176	1265	31	35
Frederick	3167	3616	445	193
Harford	1527	1862	82	81
Howard	530	830	189	1
Kent	694	852	74	42
Montgomery	1125	1155	99	50
Prince George's	1048	885	43	1
Queen Anne's	879	908	87	00
Somerset	1339	1536	89	2
St. Mary's	920	261	190	1
Talbot	898	793	98	2
Washington	2475	2567	283	95
Worcester	1425	1048	90	00
	42,482	41,760	5,966	2,294

Breckinridge's plurality over Bell, 722.

Left: Presidential election results, 1860. *From the* Baltimore Sun.

Below: Census map of slave population, Howard County, 1860. *U.S. Census Bureau.*

characteristics. They inherit, among other things, a mania for politics, perpetuated by events in an almost riotous political past, and constantly aggravated by bitter factional strife.[150]

That HoCo was part of the South explains some of the attitudes that have persisted over the years. The Library of Congress has a "map showing the distribution of the slave population of the southern states of the United States compiled from the census of 1860." It is stark to see how similar HoCo looks to the southern counties like Calvert and Charles, helping us to understand that HoCo's history had more in common with its southern neighbors. Think about this as you read about the experiences of some of the Black families of HoCo.

THE MARYLAND STATE COLONIZATION SOCIETY

Looking back at the early history of HoCo, and Maryland, one can get the impression that folks didn't want Black people living there for one reason or another. In all fairness, there were perhaps many people, especially in the northern states, who genuinely felt that emigration to Africa was the best thing for their Black neighbors because they thought Black people would be free to govern themselves as true equals there, something they did not see as possible in the United States. There were many impassioned pleas to figure out how to end slavery and return African Americans to their "native home," although there were generations born here that only knew Maryland and the United States as home.

However, the intent was clearly to remove all Black people and make Maryland an all-White state and a model for the rest of the country to follow. One of the first acts of former governor George Howard (he served from July 8, 1831, to January 17, 1833) was to sign into law two bills that were racist and favored slaveholders of the state, one of which established the Maryland State Colonization Society.[151] There was a competing movement designed by the Black population, for the Black population, promoting emigration to Haiti, a place where White people were disallowed and which was seen as more acceptable than the colonization movement to most Black leaders.[152]

Chapter 281 of the 1831 Maryland laws, called "An Act Relating to the People of Color in This State," was passed on March 12, 1832. This act established the Maryland State Colonization Society (MSCS) with a board of managers "whose duty shall be to remove from the state of Maryland, the people of color now free, and such as shall hereafter become so, to the colony of Liberia, in Africa."[153] This was to be done with their consent, although Section 4 of the act states,

> *That in case any slave or slaves so manumitted* [legally set free] *cannot be removed without separating families, and the said slave or slaves so unwilling on that account to be removed, shall desire to renounce the freedom so intended by the deed or will, then it shall and may be competent to such slave or slaves, to renounce, in open court, the benefit of said deed or will, and continue to be a slave.*[154]

So if someone was going to be freed by manumission via a deed or will and didn't want to be sent to Liberia without their family, then they could renounce their freedom and remain a slave. It is not known if this actually happened or how many instances of this situation arose, because records are sparse and there has been little research on the topic.

It is clear the purpose of the MSCS was to rid Maryland of free Blacks. In fact, Chapter 323 of the Maryland laws, passed on March 14, 1832, and signed by Governor Howard, called "An Act Relating to Free Negroes and Slaves," tried to prohibit free Blacks from coming into Maryland from other states. It stated that "no free negro or mulatto shall immigrate to, or settle in this state."[155] This was how the people who held power in Maryland felt. There was a problem, and they needed to figure out a way to solve it.

Once the MSCS was active with a board of managers, it published its official statements in documents and in the press. One of MSCS's statements left no doubt of the society's intent, although it later made a claim that it was primarily in favor of the abolition of slavery: "The evil of an increasing black population is pressing upon us, and the longer that we delay to adopt measures to check it, the greater does the task become....The resources of the state are now amply sufficient for the removal of the whole of her free coloured population, as well as of all those slaves who may be manumitted with the view of colonization."[156]

The MSCS remained active for a number of years and published reports of its progress. According to the *Maryland Colonization Journal* of January 1856 (vol. 8, no. 8) the board of managers of the MSCS met on January 4, 1856, and reported that

- a total of 1,212 free Blacks emigrated from Maryland to Liberia

- a total of 4,877 enslaved people were manumitted and may have been sent to Liberia
  - 1,839 manumissions were immediate
  - 3,038 were prospective or conditional

There were 1,025 emigrants and 5,571 manumissions documented between 1831 and 1851, but that still doesn't answer the question of exactly how many people emigrated. However, in a census in November 1852, there was a list of 785 residents of "Maryland in Liberia," a decrease from the 804 residents counted during a census of 1849 and the 757 counted in the census of 1848.[157]

The Maryland State Archives (MSA), in its overview document of the Maryland State Colonization Society, further states: "In a report to the society's board of managers, travelling agent John H. Kennard unironically summarized many of the key reasons that blacks opposed colonization."

> *They* [free Blacks] *are taught to believe, and, do believe, that this is their country, their home. A Country and home, now wickedly withholden from them but which they will presently possess, own and control. Those who Emigrate to Liberia, are held up to the world, as the vilest and veriest traitors to their race, and especially so, towards their brethren in bonds. Every man woman and child who leaves this country for Africa is considered one taken from the strength of the colored population and by his departure, as protracting the time when the black man will by the strength of his own arm compel those who despise and oppress him, to acknowledge his rights, redress his wrongs, and restore the wages, long due and iniquitously withholden.*[158]

We hope we can learn from this terrible time in history. To hide or ignore these facts is to erase the state of the world that led us to where we are today.

Early Black Landowners

Black home ownership in HoCo began earlier than many think, as is shown in the book *Early Ellicott City Black History*.[159] Myths are busted in this book about Black history in the county seat and the true origin and story of the log cabin that was on Merryman Street before it was moved to Main Street for "show and tell" and used as a prop for press conferences. Blacks owned land in Ellicott Mills, and some were prominent citizens of their time before 1850, but in Guilford, land ownership by Black people didn't appear to start until right after the Civil War. Thomas Fisher, another Black landowner who lived in Baltimore County, also owned land in Ellicott Mills. By 1834, he owned the land in old Ellicott Mills that Levi Gillis lived on before the latter purchased it in 1851. Based on the 1850 census, four Black men owned land in Ellicott Mills, and at least fifteen others, almost half of whom were women, owned land in the rest of Howard District. George Johnson, a cooper in Ellicott Mills, stood out with a $2,500 land value—more than most of the folks in Howard District.[160] By the 1860 census, in which Howard District was now HoCo, Black land ownership in the rural county had greatly increased. But in Ellicott Mills, George Johnson, the cooper, was the only Black person listed as owning land.[161]

Back in Guilford, the purchase of land by the First Baptist Church of Guilford in 1903 and Willis Carter's farmland purchase in 1904 were crucial for the development of the community.[162] But we were curious about when the very first Black landowners came to Guilford. While Black families owned land in Ellicott City and elsewhere before the Civil War, it appears that was not the case in Guilford until well after the war was over. Henry Penny, a local White farmer and landowner, was the critical connection to begin land and home ownership for Black families.[163]

Deed from Henry Penny to William Watkins, 1866. *MSA*.

In 1866, Henry and Elizabeth Penny sold just over four acres to William Watkins from within the land patent Jones Fancy. In 1869, Henry and Elizabeth Penny sold another seven acres of land within Jones Fancy to Daniel Boston, a farm laborer. Boston took a mortgage from George W. Marlow and then sold the land back to Marlow in 1873 for the same price as the mortgage. According to the 1900 census, Wesley Watkins still owned his home, as did the Boston family, who had relocated closer to the Savage/Annapolis Junction area by then. Boston was a trustee for about thirty years for the Annapolis Junction "colored" school near Asbury Church, starting in 1886.

In the 1910 census, Isabella Boston, Mollie Thomas, Carrie Moore, Charles Green Jr., John Holland, Mary Carter (Willis's widow), James Carter, Elizabeth Harding, Nicholas Boston, William Oliver, Charles Green Sr., James Curtis and George Curtis were all listed as Black homeowners in Guilford. These families were the founders of the historically Black community of Guilford.

Freetown and Worthington

Freetown is an area not far from Guilford along the original Guilford Road. It has been associated with an area where the formerly enslaved men and women of Nicolas Worthington settled. The area in Simpsonville was part of 150 acres of land that Worthington set aside for just seventeen of the many he enslaved to live on.[164] Since enslavers paid taxes on their "property," sometimes they would free those they enslaved through the process of manumission, particularly after their deaths. This way, their families, or estate executors, avoided paying that tax. Sometimes, manumissions were truly for the benefit of the enslaved, as their time of servitude may have ended or an enslaver would grant freedom because they believed it was the right thing to do.

Nicholas Worthington (1770–1845), son of John Worthington the Elder, a wealthy landowner, inherited lands from both his father and his brother Thomas. Nicholas Worthington was also an investor and businessman, a justice of the peace and a founding commissioner of the Patapsco Bank of Maryland in 1835 along with Thomas B. Dorsey, Charles Carroll of Homewood and Charles W. Dorsey, among others. Worthington named Dorsey executor of his estate in his 1845 will.[165]

Freetown land patent map. *Author's collection.*

Worthington provided for those he enslaved through manumission and gave seventeen of them a life estate, meaning they could live on the land but would not own it. His will mentioned "150 acres of land, being part of the tract of land called 'Worthington's Improvement' or of 'Athol Enlarged,'" which ended up solely on Worthington's Improvement.[166]

Worthington died on November 13, 1845, and between his will and inventory, it appears he manumitted about forty-seven of those he had enslaved. While seventeen of them were provided for with life estates, they did not own the land and could not pass it down to their children. Of the forty-seven formerly enslaved, he provided cash to thirty-one of them, ranging from $30 for most of them up to $2,000 for one in particular. Sixteen of them received no cash or land on which to live. News of the will establishing freedom through manumission for those Worthington enslaved spread across the country and even to London. Headlines included "Emancipation by Will" and "Noble Example," lauding Worthington's last acts.[167]

However, not everyone Worthington planned to manumit was freed. Three enslaved children listed in Worthington's will inventory were sold instead. Gustavus, age nine, was sold to William Clark, and Nell and Jenny, ages ten and eight, were sold to T.W. Ligon, a future governor of Maryland; the sale was recorded on February 1, 1848. A photocopy of this sale is in Beulah Buckner's records. Researcher Marlena Jareaux found the official court record at the MSA, which she documented on her website I Am

Louisa, about the experiences of a young Black girl in Maryland during this same period and her struggle to keep her freedom.[168]

Ownership of the 150 acres of land was passed down to William Clarke to hold for his son John Ridgely Clarke, per Worthington's will. Worthington was extremely close to the Clarkes and generous to them in his will. Five of the seventeen enslaved men, women and children manumitted were clearly living along Old Guilford Road, now called Harriet Tubman Lane, just five years later, according to the 1850 census of the Howard District of AACo.[169] In particular, Abraham and Patience Dorsey, Isaac and Nelly Holland and Henry and Airy (possibly) Baker were living in their three independent households but did not own the land on which they lived. Isaac Holland was one of the original trustees at the Locust Church.

Another household next to the Hollands was occupied by Airy Johnson (age sixty) and Kitty Brooks (fifty-eight). Johnson and Brooks were among the surnames used by those Worthington enslaved. There was not always a clear first and last name of the enslaved individuals in the will, but it is likely that Johnson and Brooks were also manumitted by the Worthington will. Similarly, living next to Henry Baker were Benjamin, Hamilton and Lucy Johnson and Rachel Johnson and Matilda Cooke. Four members of a Cook family were manumitted, so it is possible that these other two families were also formerly enslaved.[170] On Simon Martenet's 1860 map, the households of A. Johnson, R. Dorsey, I. Holland and A. Dorsey are all listed along Guilford Road, east of Simpsonville.[171]

Although those formerly enslaved by Worthington did not end up owning their land, they still experienced a remarkable journey from enslavement to freedom on the land of their former enslaver.

THE INSURRECTION OF AUGUSTUS COLLINS

Augustus Worthington Collins was born around 1830, when the Maryland State Colonization Society formed. Collins was one of those enslaved from birth, as was his family, by Thomas Worthington (son of John), who was Nicholas Worthington's brother. His mother, Fanny, and sister Ellen were freed in May 1843 on the death of Thomas Worthington, per his will. Worthington, who had no wife or children, left his plantation where he had lived, called Worthington's Improvement, to his brother Nicholas.[172]

Collins was not manumitted for his freedom until 1852, when he was about twenty-two years old.[173] Those enslaved by Thomas Worthington

Claudius Steward — Clopar

Names of Slaves	No	Age	Sex	Physical Condition	Slave for	Enlisted	Drafted	Name & date of Regiment	Compensation From State	From U S
William Barne	1	41	male	Healthy	Life					
Isiah Brown	2	20	"	"	"					
Alexander Green	3	16	"	"	"					
Samuel Green	4	15	"	"	"					
Albert Boston	5	8	"	"	22 years					
Rodolphus Boston	6	3	"	"	27 "					
Samuel Boston	7	1	"	"	29 "					
Joshua Conway	8	9	"	"	Life					
John Badger	9	26	"	"	8 years					
David Hopkins	10	2	"	"	Life					
Charles A. Hopkins	11	1	"	"	"					
Fanny Hopkins	12	52	female	"	"					
Clear Hopkins	13	21	"	"	"					
Clarissa Hopkins	14	19	"	"	"					
Sarah Hopkins	15	15	"	"	"					
Caroline Badger	16	28	"	"	8 years					
Mary A. Boston	17	28	"	"	2 "					
Emma Boston	18	5	"	"	25 "					

Test: Mary E Browning
Mary Cook   See have Oct 1868

Slave statistics for Claudius Steward for potential compensation, 1868. *MSA.*

were not to be freed until reaching twenty-one for men and sixteen for women, according to his will. After being manumitted, it is not certain where Augustus lived. In 1850, his parents and siblings likely lived in the "Freetown" area in election District Five on the west side of what is now Route 29, as they did in 1860.[174]

April 1861 was a tumultuous time for our area. While the first shots of the Civil War were fired a long way away in Fort Sumter, South Carolina, preparations for a war occurred right here with the fear of insurrection by the enslaved.

Within a week following the Battle of Fort Sumter, President Lincoln called for the Union army to travel to Washington to protect the Capitol. Troops from Pennsylvania traveling through Baltimore were met with violence from the Confederate sympathizers, and Baltimore's Mayor Brown warned President Lincoln not to send any more troops through his town. A volunteer militia from Massachusetts that had to change train lines in Baltimore to reach Washington faced rocks and bullets from the mob. The altercation resulted in four Union soldiers dead and three dozen wounded, along with the deaths of eleven rioters. Our state song, "Maryland, My Maryland," was written as a poem to sympathize with the rioters and their Confederate cause.[175]

Insurrections within Maryland and HoCo caused great fear among plantation owners and farmers whose businesses depended on the enslaved. There were still dozens of enslaved people working as farm laborers throughout the greater Guilford area, mostly focused on the farms north of Murray Hill and Berger Roads. In fact, in July 1861, there was an alleged planned insurrection led by Augustus Collins. The *Baltimore Sun* reported that "a family of free negroes named Collins, consisting of the mother, two daughters, and two sons, who reside in the neighborhood of Savage Factory, have been committed to jail at Ellicott's Mills, charged with plotting an insurrection of the slaves in that vicinity."[176]

In September 1861, a grand jury determined there was enough evidence to arrest Collins for "raising an insurrection" on July 23.[177] When they went to arrest him, he and his family resisted, and they were then also accused of assault and resisting arrest. Those arrested included Collins, his younger brother, Richard, and his sisters, Ellen Bell and Mary.[178]

Collins was the primary target of the charges. In a September hearing, Collins requested his trial be moved outside of HoCo for fear that an "impartial trial cannot be had in court here."[179] The court agreed to move his trial to Annapolis in Anne Arundel County. The Circuit Court for Anne Arundel County convened on January 27, 1862, on the case "charged with inciting a Negro insurrection, assault with intent to kill, and also for rioting."[180]

Collins requested to represent himself and was granted permission to serve as his own counsel. The *Baltimore Sun* reported that

> *a posse were summoned to effect his arrest, when he called to his assistance his father and several sisters who challenged the authority or courage of the officers and their posse to make the arrest. Finally, the whole party were arrested and taken to Ellicott's Mills and lodged in jail, after which one of the sisters* [Mary] *was tried and convicted and sentenced to imprisonment in the HoCo jail for several months.*[181]

Collins was found not guilty of two of the three charges: assault with intent to kill and resisting arrest. However, he was found guilty of "attempting to raise an insurrection" and was sentenced to be sold into slavery for a period of seven years. He was fortunate not to have been found guilty of an actual insurrection, which was punishable by death by hanging. Collins was to be sold on March 18 and sent out of state to serve his seven-year sentence as an enslaved man.[182]

PUBLIC SALE —The undersigned will offer for sale, at the Court House in the city of Annapolis, at 12 o'clock M. on TUESDAY, the 18th March, 1862, a NEGRO MAN, named AUGUSTUS COLLINS, aged about forty-five years; said negro having been convicted at the October term of the Circuit Court for Anne Arundel county for inciting an insurrection and sentenced to be sold as a slave, for seven years, out of the State, from the 9th of March, 1862. Terms cash, by order of the court.
WM. BRYAN, Sheriff.
Annapolis, 10th March, 1862.   m13 6t!

Public sale notice for Augustus Collins, 1862. *From the* Baltimore Sun.

The silver lining to this story is that to meet the quotas for enlistment into the Union army and navy, many enslaved men were "recruited" to serve. The governor of Maryland appointed a couple of commissioners for meeting the enlistment quotas in the state—one of whom was Frederick Fickey Jr. Fickey was responsible for freeing Collins, who then enlisted in the navy in Wilmington, Delaware, on November 26, 1862. Collins served on the USS *Patapsco* as an officer's steward in 1863, after which he returned to HoCo for about four years and then moved on to Washington, D.C., and Montgomery County.[183] In 1875, he served briefly on the USS *Relief*.[184]

Collins was thought to have died in 1883, the victim of a robbery while working as a messenger for Wells Fargo. In her pension testimony, Collins's wife described her husband as having been born a slave to Thomas Worthington and, after being discharged from the navy, working on the Worthington Farm near Simpsonville for four years, then spending three years in Washington, D.C., farming and living with his sister-in-law Anna Sewell. They had a restaurant on K Street for three years and, in 1880, went west working for Fickey. That was the last time she ever saw him. He wrote to her from Colorado and then Idaho, sending money each time. She received money from him until July 1883 and presumed he was dead after that.[185]

This is an amazing story about a family in and out of enslavement and resistance who made a decent life—folks from right in our own backyard.

Harriet Tubman Slept Here—or Did She?

Harriet Tubman, a true American hero from the Eastern Shore of Maryland, is documented to have made thirteen trips from 1850 to 1860 to guide about seventy relatives and friends from the Eastern Shore, including her siblings, to freedom in Philadelphia and on to Canada. She joined the Civil War effort in South Carolina as a nurse, cook, scout and spy for the Union.

With the former Harriet Tubman School building now converted into a cultural center in the area once called Freetown, it is understandable that Howard Countians promote stories of Harriet Tubman's visits to our area. Stories of Tubman's exploits in HoCo first appeared in a 1994 Maryland Historical Trust Inventory form, then in a local book and on the websites of history nonprofit organizations in the county:

> *Once upon a time a log cabin stood on this spot of ground adjacent to the Deep Run…a resting and stopping off place for Harriet Tubman where she could obtain water and food. Where she was safe, secure and protected, until she could reach the cemetery near freetown road.*[186]

> *Locust Cemetery—Oral History says that Harriet Tubman and fleeing slaves hid and rested at the gravesites. The Cemetery is located at the corner of Harriet Tubman Lane and Freetown Road.*[187]

> *The area on which Columbia is now located provided means of escape to those held in bondage. Harriet Tubman was able to pass through Freetown, where the African American population was free.*[188]

Fact versus fiction. But are these stories really true? No oral history sources, or any other sources, have been found, and the "heritage" approach to history continued and has been repeated often. Our experience with this heritage approach is that it "accentuates the positive but sifts away what is problematic."[189] But these positive stories we hold dear must still be fact-checked to best honor those mentioned. There was no reason for Harriet Tubman to even be in Howard County and no evidence that the Middle Patuxent River or the Freetown area was ever used as a route for Harriet Tubman for the Underground Railroad. We know there were enslaved people who escaped from this area, but there is no documented escape route (yet), particularly dealing with the tiny Middle Patuxent River that would have led in both directions to slave plantations.

Some of the difficulties in these accounts include the fact that in the 1850s, only a few free Black families lived in the Freetown area and were surrounded by plantations and farms using enslaved workers. In addition, Locust Church (then known as Locust Chappel [sic]) does not appear to have existed until land was obtained in 1868 and dedicated to it in 1869, well after the Civil War, when Harriet Tubman was living in the state of New York, so her having slept in a cemetery on that land is highly unlikely.[190] There was no known cemetery there prior to this time, and in fact, in the 1980s, African American researcher Beulah Buckner found that the earliest grave marker dated to 1901, although there certainly could have been earlier ones.[191]

The Middle Patuxent River was also not a route to safer lands in the north, as traveling upstream would have taken freedom seekers through the largest populations of enslaved people in Howard County (e.g., Charles Carroll of Carrolton's lands), and similarly, going downstream would also result in traveling through plantations with enslaved workers. Neither route led to freedom, which would have been toward Baltimore and beyond.

Elkridge is so much closer to routes of freedom than Freetown that the story of Harriet Tubman being at Elkridge and then traveling to Freetown would have resulted in her going in the wrong direction. Elkridge Landing and the railroads, and Deep Creek, were likely routes that escaped slaves took. The MHT form HO-639 contains an example of oral history passed down within a family, but much of it is in error, lending no credence to the story of Harriet Tubman visiting that area. In fact, the author of the form erroneously thought his ancestor William Henry Howard was enslaved by John Eager Howard's family, but there is no evidence for this claim. In fact, William Henry Howard was born a free man; his 1856 certificate of freedom was mistaken for proof of enslavement.[192]

So did Harriet Tubman travel through Howard County as described above? Without any evidence to support these accounts, and with evidence to the contrary, the answer would have to be no. Did enslaved men, women and children escape from slavery in these areas? It is very likely, and this topic deserves to be more thoroughly researched, as do those individuals who may have been involved with the Underground Railroad. There is more history to discover.

To learn more about this topic, *Seeking Freedom: A History of the Underground Railroad in Howard County* is a worthwhile book to check out and isn't dependent on the stories of Harriet Tubman visiting. This book provides elements of history rarely discussed in Howard County and is worth reading, learning and teaching.[193] While Howard County would love to count Harriet Tubman among the honored guests of this county, we cannot make that claim. But we should still learn and teach about this incredible American hero born on the Eastern Shore of Maryland.

Jim Crow: Born and Bred in Howard County

The flames of racial discrimination after the Civil War were fanned quite well here in HoCo. Jim Crow, originally a persona of a popular minstrel show performer, started to become popular in the 1830s as a derogatory expression for people of color.

Born and raised in HoCo, Arthur Pue Gorman served as U.S. senator for Maryland from 1881 to 1899 and again from 1903 to 1906. Gorman's father, Peter, a contractor for the B&O constructing its Washington Branch line, owned two slaves (sixty and seventeen years old) and his mother, Elizabeth A. Brown (her maiden name), owned fourteen slaves aged between two and twenty-four years old.[194] Since Gorman, as a nine-year-old, lived with his parents, it is natural he would have been supported and raised by these enslaved people on their plantation. But this is not what distinguished his association with oppression.

Through his father's political connections, Gorman became a shrewd and formidable politician and served as a U.S. senator from 1881 to 1899 and again from 1903 until his death in 1906. After the Fifteenth Amendment was ratified in 1870, the Black vote was mostly against Gorman's Democratic political party and in favor of the party of Lincoln. As the Black vote grew, there was concern that it would tip the balance of elections to the Republicans. Gorman lost the vote in 1889 and was desperate to return to the Senate.

A.P. Gorman knew in 1901 that any proposed amendment to Maryland's constitution would be legally challenged if it singled out disenfranchisement of just Black voters. So he supported the Poe Amendment, which mandated literacy tests that would disqualify many more Blacks than Whites as voters.

We found nothing written about Gorman's views on race before he threw his support behind the Poe Amendment. Desiring a return to the U.S. Senate, he devised a plan that would disenfranchise all illiterate voters, which was passed by the Maryland legislature in 1901. The new Maryland election law would not allow party emblems or images on ballots and would provide no assistance to voters. Michael Walsh of Carroll County voted for the bill, explaining,

I believe, sir, that white men should govern in this state....I believe the presence of 55,000 negro voters in this State, 26,600 of whom are illiterate and ignorant, is a menace to the progress and well-being of this State, and a dangerous condition which much be met at some time, and the sooner the better. [195]

Gorman narrowly won reelection in 1901, and by the time he took office in 1903 (there was over a year's delay in those days), he had worked on broader disenfranchisement of the illiterate voter through an amendment to the Maryland constitution. It is his public political record on just this issue, the Poe Amendment to the Maryland constitution, and his own words in the early 1900s and his support for the disenfranchisement of the Black voter that put him in a negative light. Senator Gorman's views are noted in these three quotes from 1903:

I said then, as I say now, that this country was made by the white men, that the Anglo-Saxons made its laws and its Constitution, that they conquered first the Indians and then the English, and that no other race of men shall ever have possession of this state or this country. [196]

No greater crime against good government, nor greater outrage against the white women of our land has ever been perpetrated than the enfranchisement by constitutional amendment of the negro. [197]

From the day a cargo of Africans was landed and sold as slaves until this hour the burden of the white men of this county had been greater than that borne by any people known to history....The Anglo-Saxon has never and will never tolerate the social equality or the political domination of the negro race. [198]

In a speech at Ellicott City in October 1905 to support the Poe Amendment to disenfranchise the Black voter, Gorman said:

Experience has shown that in States where it [the understanding clause] *is in force there is not an intelligent white man, naturalized or native, who has not passed the examination without the slightest trouble, and there is not one negro in twenty of the field class that can have an idea of what the Constitution is if you read it to him three times.* [199]

Gorman supported another lifelong Howard Countian, Edwin Warfield, for governor in 1902. In his gubernatorial acceptance speech in 1903, Warfield said,

> Therefore I take my stand firmly upon that plank in the platform of our party which declares that the "political destinies of Maryland should be shaped and controlled by the white people of the State." And I appeal to all citizens, irrespective of party, who love and honor the State, to lend their earnest and active support in this contest for the supremacy of the white race, for the cause of civilization and good government.[200]

Warfield did not like the literacy test for White voters in the Poe Amendment. He preferred the Straus Amendment, which focused only on disenfranchising Black voters. Neither amendment would become law. Governor Warfield, who has a major road named after him in downtown Columbia, later said:

> The people of Southern Maryland and the Eastern Shore counties, where the ignorant negro vote is so large as to threaten white supremacy and good government, have always had my most earnest sympathy and I have always stood ready to come to their aid with every proper and legitimate method.…I declared in favor of eliminating the ignorant and thriftless negro voter in Maryland, and upon that declaration I was elected.[201]

While governor, Warfield was able to enact a Jim Crow railroad car law in 1904 "to provide separate cars or coaches for white and colored passengers, without discrimination in the quality or convenience or accommodation in such cars or coaches."[202] It is not surprising that Warfield had contempt for the "thriftless negro," as he was a Lost Cause sympathizer raised by slaves in a southern-sympathizing family—and especially because two of his brothers fought as Confederates in the Civil War with one suffering death as a prisoner of war.

The son of enslavers, Warfield may have been too young to legally own property, but he greatly benefited from the servitude of those enslaved, who met his every need until the end of slavery, when he was just over sixteen years old. He knew how to "boss the job." Even in later years, those formerly enslaved still referred to him as "Massa Edwin," demonstrating his lifelong status in their eyes. Then again, everyone knew who the boss was. Warfield felt that "the real slaves were the master and mistress, who

Edwin Warfield "bossing the job," 1911. *From the* Baltimore Sun.

were charged with the entire responsibility and care, while the servants had all their wants provided for."[203]

HoCo born and raised politicians were some of the most pro–Jim Crow people around. This is what is meant by systemic oppression—it comes from the people in power.

Chapter 7

PUBLIC EDUCATION IN HOWARD COUNTY

Public schools didn't start until 1865, as required by the Maryland Constitution of 1864. But the new state board of education would be put in control of the local schools, which was not well received by the counties. So in 1867, the latest Maryland Constitution placed control back under the counties and the City of Baltimore while maintaining taxes to support schools and allowing all students to receive a basic education.[204]

Educating the White population was the priority, using up almost all of the allocated tax base and funding. The state board of education recommended amendments to state law that included establishing separate schools for Black children.[205] "Schools for Colored Children" was finally included as a requirement in the Public School Law of Maryland, passed in 1872.

Education for Black children had already started in HoCo with the help of benevolent associations such as the Baltimore Association for the Moral and Educational Improvement of the Colored People and the New England Freedmen's Aid Society. The U.S. Freedmen's Bureau, created by Congress in 1865, continued the work already being done by the War Department.[206]

Freedmen's Bureau records note that in 1864, Thomas Hood was provided $600 "for one stone building and out-houses" for a large school that had already been purchased by the school's Black trustees. This building was the former Warfield Academy in Cooksville.[207] This may be why some researchers erroneously thought, when the Warfield Academy was operating in the late 1840s, before its bankruptcy, that it was built for African American students.

Reports show that most of the funding for these schools was provided by the freed people themselves, including tuition. By 1867, "colored schools" in HoCo existed in Cooksville, Elkridge Landing and Ellicott City, teaching hundreds of formerly enslaved and free children and some adults. The exact locations of the schools at Elkridge and Ellicott City have not been determined, but in 1869, it was reported that the Elkridge school was in a church. In 1871, the Ellicott City school was called the "Mission School" owned by "the people," with twenty-six of the thirty-eight students free before the Civil War.[208] It is possible that this school was located in Missionary Bottom on Merryman Lane in the heart of Ellicott City's Black community.

"RAILROAD" CARROLL

One of our earliest teachers, J.T.R.R. Carroll, sometimes known as "John Railroad Carroll" because of his initials, has been described as one of HoCo's "picturesque and venerable characters."[209] Carroll was born in HoCo in 1838 and was the oldest son of Thomas and Cena Carroll. In the 1850 census, his father was listed as a sixty-year-old pauper, which is probably why Carroll ended up in the Thompson household with his younger brothers and sisters by 1860. He started his early work life farming and then was employed as a brakeman for the B&O Railroad. In 1865, when he was twenty-seven, he was listed among the first official teachers in HoCo, the same year that the Maryland Teachers Association was initiated.[210]

Carroll moved to Guilford shortly after he began teaching. In 1878, a new public school was built there, where Carroll taught until he retired in June 1901 at sixty-three years of age after thirty-five years of teaching. In 1904, the Maryland Teacher's Pension Law was

List Starts With 37.

Thirty-seven were decided to be worthy of the pension, nine applications were found defective and two were rejected. The following will be the first names upon the list of retired public school teachers:

SAMUEL J. TAMMANY, Havre de Grace.
MISS ALICE M. DAWLEY, Baltimore.
MISS SARA S. RICE, Baltimore.
MISS NANCY W. SMITH, Baltimore.
MISS MARTHA BIDDLE, Elkton.
MISS ELLEN M. CLARKE, Cumberland.
JOHN OTHO HAYES, Wolfesville.
MISS MARY E. CLARKE, Davis, W. Va.
J. T. R. R. CARROLL, Guilford.
JOHN H. R. McCARTHY, McConnics.
HORACE TELL, Drury.
JOHN LANDERS, Thurmont.
B. F. HAYNES, Marion.
MISS ELIZA ADAMS, Baltimore.
MISS SARAH N. WATERS, Watersville.
MISS ELIZA E. FISH, Salisbury.
MISS LOTTA J. FISH, Salisbury.
MISS LAURA A. YEATMAN, Baltimore.
MISS MARY EMMA NORRIS, Singer.
W. H. P. BRYAN, Madison.
WILLIAM H. PAGE, Washington Grove.
ROBERT F. DODSON, Waterbury.
JOHN W. POSEY, Wicomico.
THOMAS TIPTON, Hampstead.
JOHN F. NEFF, Cumberland.
ALFRED TUCKER, SR., Centreville.
WILLIAM L. FLEAGLE, Frizzellburg.
JAMES M. KREIDLER, Maplesville.
JOHN H. BEAUCHAMP, Fairmount.
FRANCIS KENNEY, Baltimore county.
JOHN S. STANSBURY, Arlington.
FRANKLIN L. KING, Williamsport.
JOHN E. KELLEY, Hagerstown.
GEORGE W. HICKS, Hicksville.
JEREMIAH SPICER, Taylor's Island.
MISS SARAH V. METTEE, Baltimore.
CHARLES A. LE COMPTE, Cambridge.

A certified copy of this list will be furnished the Comptroller immediately.

It was decided yesterday that even though a teacher has not taught since the law was passed, he or she is eligible to the pension.

Original teachers retirement list from 1902. *From the Baltimore Sun.*

reenacted, providing a pension to teachers who had spent at least twenty-five years in the classroom and who were at least sixty years old along with having a spotless record. Carroll was more than qualified and became HoCo's first teacher pensioner on August 27, 1902.[211]

Carroll was not only a teacher and family-man, but he also learned to become a surveyor and was so proficient he was elected to become county surveyor by 1879.[212] When he was announced again as a candidate in 1907, it was reported that the crowd celebrated, with one speaker referring to him as "John Thomas Railroad Carroll." In case you were curious, J.T.R.R. stands for John Thomas Ridgely Randolph.[213]

Carroll retired as county surveyor after thirty-one years in 1909 and went back to tending his farm. Although he was reported to be active and in good health, on June 18, 1923, a neighbor, Ida Collins, went to his home to deliver a telephone message and found his body in the yard near his water pump. Railroad Carroll died at the age of eighty-five.[214]

The Non-Lynching of Hezekiah Brown

While it was called the Annapolis Junction Colored School No. 2 in District Six, the school was on the Asbury Church grounds. Asbury Church was formerly a Methodist Episcopal church and was noted on the Hopkins Atlas of 1860 just west of Route 1 on Guilford Road and near Annapolis Junction. This is one of the earliest Black communities and churches in our area and had been associated with the Locust United Methodist Church in Simpsonville that was formed in 1869.[215] It was also associated with the First Baptist Church of Guilford founded by Reverend Carter. Carter's oldest son, Richard, married Dora Mack, whose parents, Cornelius and Catherine Mack, donated the land where the current Asbury United Methodist church sits.[216]

Reverend Hezekiah Brown, a preacher and teacher, was associated with the school next to the Asbury United Methodist Church for many years. Reverend Brown began his teaching career in HoCo at the school next to Asbury Church for thirteen years, from the fall of 1884 until July 1897.[217] Among the school trustees during this time were Cornelius Mack, Daniel Boston, Amos Henson and Henry Carroll. Aside from the dedication of teachers like Reverend Brown and the school trustees, the Asbury community had fine families and brought us another long-term teacher, Lorraine Arthur, who taught at the segregated Guilford schools.[218]

Not everyone was happy that the Reverend Brown was a teacher in Annapolis Junction. He was welcomed in his first year of teaching with

LATEST BY TELEGRAPH.

REPORTED LYNCHING IN MARYLAND.

A Negro School Teacher Hanged by a Mob for Living with a White Girl—Another Dynamite Explosion in London this Afternoon.

By Telegraph to THE NEW ERA.

BALTIMORE, Md., Dec. 13.—A morning paper publishes the statement that Hezekiah Brown, a colored school teacher in a lonely part of Howard county, was hanged yesterday by thirteen masked men. It is charged that he became too intimate with a young white woman whom he declared he had married, but no record of such marriage could be found. The lynching is said to have occurred in a wild section of the country, which is sparsely populated. Inquiries at Ellicott City, the county seat of Howard, fail to confirm the reported lynching. Nothing having been heard of it there, the State Attorney has sent a message to ascertain the facts.

Hezekiah Brown lynching article, 1884. *From the* Daily New Era *(Lancaster, PA)*.

reports in the newspapers that he had been lynched for having an affair with a White woman or seducing her into marriage, whatever best fit the narrative that he wasn't fit for teaching.

As lynching stories go, few are known to have a happy ending. On December 13, 1884, newspapers reported the awful lynching of Hezekiah Brown. Oddly enough, the reports included the fact that the county could not confirm that it actually happened. It was said that Brown had married a White woman, with a son, after a long relationship. However, it was a false story, likely invented by folks who were not happy about a White woman with a son attending a Black church and being educated in a school there. There were no additional problems reported after the reported lynching, and Reverend Brown had a long teaching career in HoCo. Perhaps this was the first integrated public classroom in HoCo.[219]

During his time at Asbury, Reverend Brown was active in the Colored Schoolteachers Association as well as Methodist camp meetings. One of those meetings was Douglas Day in 1891, in honor of Frederick Douglas, who would speak at HoCo's Irving Park near the Annapolis Junction train station. He was met by Hezekiah Brown and others and escorted to the camp meeting. Douglas gave a speech full of advice for those in attendance. One of the insights he shared was that "money is not exactly the root of all evil. We must acquire property, and we must leave something." He was adamant about the sobriety and industriousness of the people to acquire property to pass down to the next generation so they would have something to build on.[220]

Reverend Brown left teaching at Asbury to become the principal teacher in Ellicott City's colored school from the 1897–98 school year through the 1899–1900 school year, with Julia A. Johnson assisting. Reverend Brown joined the Anne Arundel schools starting in the 1900–01 school year at Colored School 1, District 5, again as the principal teacher.[221] He was still there for the 1904–05 school year, marking twenty years as a teacher.[222] He served as a teacher for twenty-five years.[223]

Reverend Brown continued to preach where needed and was an active member of the Maryland District Lodge of the Grand United Order of Odd Fellows, becoming the grandmaster of Maryland Odd Fellows around 1922.[224] This organization was a mutual aid society open to anyone but mostly for Blacks. One of the existing Maryland lodges states that "the practical benefits of membership assisted in defraying expenses of burial, sickness, disability, and widowhood. While no exact amounts were ensured to members, the success of the Order suggests its ability to provide a reasonable level of support to those in need."[225]

In 1927, Reverend Brown stepped down as the head of the Maryland Grand United Order of Odd Fellows, with 120 lodges and about 6,200 members.[226] While visiting the Pilgrim Baptist Church in Chicago on September 9, 1928, the Reverend Hezekiah Brown died suddenly at the age of sixty-six.[227] We highly recommend the story of Reverend Brown as told by HoCo Lynching Truth & Reconciliation Inc.[228]

GUILFORD'S ROSENWALD SCHOOL

In 1907, W.C. Phillips, the superintendent of the HoCo Board of Education, reported to the state board of education that his plans for a Colored Industrial School had not yet occurred due to "the great opposition to the education of the negro in this county."[229] But despite this great opposition, the Guilford community pushed forward to make sure the children received the education they deserved.

The first public school for Black children in Guilford began in the 1905–06 school year with a total enrollment of 133 students, 47 in the elementary grades; the lone teacher's school year salary was $144. The only probable location for this school was in the First Baptist Church of Guilford, by the Carter family property. The first trustees for this school included Reverend Willis J. Carter, John Holland and David Thomas.[230]

After the untimely passing of Reverend Willis Carter in 1906, the trustees for the 1907–08 school year included John Holland, David Thomas and a Carter (first name not listed but probably James, who was trustee for many years after this). John Holland and David Thomas were both longtime residents of Guilford as well as neighbors of the Carters. The Holland and Thomas families were farmers dating to at least the 1870s. David Thomas was a cook by trade. By the 1908–09 school year, an additional school for Black children was added in District 6, possibly at Jonestown, and the next year, the enrollment at the Guilford school dropped to a total of forty-four students, all in elementary grades.[231]

From the 1907–08 through the 1919–20 school years, the three faithful trustees of the school in Guilford were John Holland, James Carter and David Thomas. James was Reverend Carter's younger brother, who worked in the quarries as a block cutter but had moved away from the area by 1920. After James Carter moved away, Jacob Coleman was appointed as the third trustee of the Guilford school for the 1920–21 school year.[232]

Coleman was a quarry man whose family moved to Guilford in 1901. He remained dedicated to education for the children, being a school trustee until his death in 1943.[233] Thomas and Coleman were such prominent citizens in Guilford that the Coleman Thomas Road off of Oakland Mills in Guilford bears their family names. The Coleman family were original members of the First Baptist Church of Guilford, and some family members still reside in Guilford.

The time of the Maryland Granite Company brought great economic and political growth, as shown by the annual Guilford Day celebrations, which attracted thousands for sporting tournaments, games, speeches, picnics and comradery. By 1917, the Maryland Granite Company had closed, Guilford Day had ended and the other quarry activities in the area had ceased.[234] This reduction of workers and their children was one cause of a request from a delegation of Black citizens from the Sixth District on May 18, 1920, for consolidation of the schools in Annapolis Junction and Guilford.[235] This new, centrally located school needed funding.

Based on his friendship with and admiration of Booker T. Washington, Julius Rosenwald, one of the founders of Sears, Roebuck and Company, began donating funds to promote education for rural Black communities in the South. This became the Julius Rosenwald Fund by 1917 and offered hope for raising part of the funds to build "colored schools."[236] The Guilford community needed as much help as possible. When requesting a school to educate the Guilford and Annapolis Junction children, the May 1920 delegation to the school board reported that it had raised $700 from the community and could get another $800 from the Rosenwald Fund, which was the amount the fund allowed for a two-room school.[237]

By January 1922, the delegation had raised even more money and requested an additional $450 from the board toward the amount needed for constructing the school. The board approved only $225 and agreed to put out a bid for the school's construction.[238] In February 1922, the board received just one bid (of $4,400), which it decided was just too expensive to approve.[239]

TABLE 99

NUMBER OF ROOMS CONSTRUCTED AND ROSENWALD AID RECEIVED FOR COLORED SCHOOLS BUILT IN MARYLAND COUNTIES FROM 1919 TO JULY 31, 1925

COUNTY	Number of Rooms							Amount of Aid from Rosenwald Fund						
	Prior to 1920	1921	1922	1923	1924	1925	Total	Prior to 1920	1921	1922	1923	1924	1925	Total
Total.............	20	15	29	47	12	45	168	$3,800	$5,300	$9,900	$12,800	$3,700	$12,700	$48,200
Allegany...........				*8			*8							
Washington........						*8	*8							
Prince George's....			6	14	2	5	27			1,600	5,200	700	1,600	9,100
Anne Arundel......			6	1		15	22			2,400	500		5,100	8,000
Worcester.........	4	3		4	2		13	1,300	1,000		1,700	800		4,800
Montgomery........		2				8	10		800				2,700	3,500
Wicomico..........	4		5			2	11	500		2,100			700	3,300
Carroll............	1	1				1	3	350	500		400			1,250
Talbot............	6		2		1		9	500		800	400			1,700
Charles...........		4		2	3		9		1,200		1,000	800		3,000
Harford...........	1			4		1	6	400			1,400		400	2,200
Baltimore.........				8		2	10				1,500		700	2,200
Calvert...........		3			2		5		1,000			600		1,600
Frederick.........	1			6			7	350			1,500			1,850
Queen Anne's......						4	4						1,500	1,500
Caroline..........	3				*1		4	400						400
Somerset..........			6				6			1,400				1,400
Howard............			2				2			800				800
St. Mary's.........		2					2		800					800
Dorchester........			2				2			800				800
Cecil.............							0							0
Kent..............							0							0

* No Rosenwald aid received.

List of schools using Rosenwald funds. *56th Annual Report Maryland State Board of Education.*

On May 2, 1922, with $2,450 reported by the school board available, William Arthur and Samuel Carter went to the board to inform it that they could build the school for the amount already raised. Since this was not a formal bid, the board had to consult with its attorney to see if it could accept the bid. No board records have yet been found with a determination, but it is assumed the school board accepted the terms from Arthur and Carter, as the board took out a $2,000 insurance policy for the school, as reported on September 19, 1922, for the beginning of that school year.

In the end, this school, which was the first in HoCo to use these funds, was reported by the HoCo superintendent to have received $800 in Rosenwald funds, $900 in county funds, $1,000 from the Black community and $300 in gifts for a total of $3,000.[240] The Guilford Colored School on Mission and Guilford Roads was built in 1922 and was the only community in HoCo to use Rosenwald funds until 1926. The Guilford community led the way for what appear to be the other two schools to receive these funds: Cooksville and Elkridge. This former school and now private residence is in the Maryland Inventory of Historic Properties but should also be in the National Register of Historic Places.[241]

New Segregated Guilford Elementary School

Creative, hardworking, community-based, persistent people of all backgrounds founded Guilford and continue to build its legacy. It is a microcosm of the true and complicated history of HoCo. In March 1950, the school board decided it would be necessary to build a new school for Black children at Guilford. The postwar Black population of District 6 had more than doubled—a new and larger public school in Guilford was now needed.[242]

The school board at first decided to purchase and build on a ten-acre lot fronting Mission Road, half a mile away, but later decided the property would not work due to topography and other factors and finally decided to build the school on the Thomas L. Collins property, where Guilford Elementary School still operates. They originally anticipated the new Guilford school to be six classrooms at a cost of $130,000–$150,000 but later decided on a twelve-room school at a price of about $225,000 to accommodate the growth in the number of students.[243]

In September 1952, the school board made a final decision to build a new "colored" elementary school in Guilford. Elkridge, Meadowridge and Colesville schools would be combined into this new school.[244] In April 1953, the school board authorized purchase of the Collins property along Oakland Mills Road. Unfortunately, there was opposition to the new school. On May 5, just a month after the purchase was approved, the school board minutes showed the following opposition to the school site on Guilford Road:

> *A delegation of twenty-five citizens of the Sixth District of Howard County appeared before the Board. Mr. Charles Hogg, attorney representing the delegation, led the discussion. Mr. Hogg stated that the delegation objected to the use of the Collins property as a site for the new Guilford Colored School for the following reasons: 1, the colored school would lower property values in the Guilford area; 2, it would increase the colored population in the colored area; 3, the delegation was not opposing a colored school but the location of the school; 4, the Mission Road site was more desirable for a school than the Collins site.*

They just didn't want to increase the Black population. Similar objections were raised to the school board on May 18, 1953, led by Dr. Frank Shipley of Savage:

POPULATION - HOWARD COUNTY BY DISTRICT AND COLOR

Population
Statistics

Bureau of Census Data

Dist.	1940			1950			Jan. 1, 1953 Estimated		
	Total	White	Col.	Total	White	Col.	Total	White	Col.
1	3229	2745	384	4607	4047	560	4890	4400	590
2	3778	3377	404	5235	4689	546	5550	4970	580
3	1974	1622	352	2348	1893	355	2500	2120	380
4	2410	1950	460	2828	2236	592	3000	2370	630
5	2304	1774	530	2551	1956	595	2700	2070	630
6	3408	2903	577	5550	4340	1210	5860	4580	1280
Total	17175	13361	2804	23119	19261	3858	24500	20410	4090

Top: HoCo population by election district, 1940s–1950s. *HoCo BOE.*

Bottom: Guilford School's first graduating class in 1956. *Courtesy of Guilford Elementary School.*

Dr. Shipley stated that several members of the delegation had called on the Superintendent on Friday, May 15, to voice their objection to the use of the Collins property as a site for the new Guilford Colored School. Dr. Shipley further stated that the Superintendent of Schools had requested the delegation to voice their objections to the Board at its next meeting. Dr. Shipley stated that the delegation wished to go on record as opposing the Guilford site for the following reasons: 1, the Crone site on the Mission Road would be more desirable because of its location near the colored population; 2, citizens in the community object to the colored school being built on the Collins site; 3, some of the large taxpayers of the sixth district feel that the school site is too close to their property and, therefore, would lower property values; 4, the proposed site is very close to the new Episcopal Church Rectory and Hall.

The school board felt that such a school would be too large and visible to be put on the small dirt Mission Road compared to the hard-surfaced and easily accessible Oakland Mills Road.

By the July 1 deadline, there were nine bids to build the "Guilford Consolidated Colored School," and the contract was awarded to Kahn Engineering Company for $216,278. Construction began by August. In March 1954, it was decided that the new Guilford Elementary School would be ready to open in September, and the school board authorized the sale of the sites of the Guilford, Colesville, Elkridge and Meadowridge schools, which would be closed and consolidated into the new school.[245]

The new Guilford Elementary School was planned in 1950 and finally opened in September 1954 as a segregated school, just four months after the Supreme Court ruling of *Brown vs. the Board of Education* stating that racial segregation in public schools was unlawful in the United States. As at the old Guilford Elementary School on Mission Road, the same trustees, Remus Dorsey, Roger Dorsey and Samuel Moore, continued at the new school on Oakland Mills Road. But it was the Guilford Elementary PTA that carried

Guilford Elementary School in 1955. *From the* Baltimore Afro American.

a loud voice on behalf of their school and pushed desegregation in HoCo. The Guilford community and their school PTA worked hard in the following years to desegregate the schools in HoCo, but for the time being, this new Guilford Elementary School was still segregated.

SEGREGATION TO INTEGRATION

The June 1954 school board meeting was business as usual for the "colored" schools as the Maryland attorney general's office needed time to reflect on the "full implications" of the Supreme Court decision, which they expected in the fall. However, the board at its June meeting wrote:

> *The laws of Maryland specifically provide for segregation in the public schools and in the teachers colleges. In view of this law requiring segregation, no program of integration can be put into effect until the decision of the Supreme Court becomes final and an effective date is set by the Supreme Court.*[246]

At their June 7, 1955 meeting, the HoCo school board acknowledged that the Supreme Court had clarified its ruling on May 31, 1955, and that segregation of public schools was clearly unlawful. All district courts and school boards were to immediately work toward desegregation "with all deliberate speed." In response to the Supreme Court clarification, the HoCo school board on June 7, 1955, made the following statement, showing no interest in pursuing desegregation quickly:

> *The Howard County Board of Education discussed the Supreme Court's opinion on the public school segregation cases and the many problems confronting the Board because of the Court's decision. There are problems relating to personnel, school plant, transportation, and the administration of the school system which need clarification under the ruling. Due to the magnitude of the problem and its many implications, the Board decided it was not wise under the circumstances to make any judgments or decisions until further study can be made.*

Ellicott City, Cooksville, Highland and Guilford were the remaining segregated colored schools, and this caused a problem for the county. There was still a strong sentiment among some who wanted to fight desegregation, as seen by a petition signed by about thirty-six thousand Marylanders and presented to the HoCo board opposing it.[247] The integration of HoCo schools would take a long time, and even in the schools that were integrated, segregated busing still occurred.

On August 16, 1955, the HoCo school board issued a formal statement that punted the issue down the road because "the detailed mechanics of this transition are up to the local authorities, in this case, the Board of Education of HoCo. The Supreme Court requires only a prompt and reasonable start toward full compliance, recognizing the problem that exists when a social system and a way of life are changed."[248]

One could write a book on the following decade of desegregating the schools. But we should recognize the outspoken efforts of the Guilford PTA and the First Baptist Church of Guilford in 1956 in supporting immediate desegregation and the HoCo NACCP and those in the community fighting for it in the following decade, like Dr. Silas E. Craft Sr.

On June 13, 1964, the HoCo school board minutes record plans for the Guilford Elementary School to be the last school desegregated in the county, in 1967.

> *In order to plan for total desegregation, the Secretary requested The Board to consider a new program. He stated that after carefully considering all of the factors involved, he recommended the following program for the next four years beginning June 30, 1964:…*
>
> *f) The Guilford Elementary School will be desegregated on June 30, 1967, and pupils may be transferred to or from this school in September, 1967, consistent with transportation policies.*

Fortunately, seemingly because of pressure brought by the HoCo NAACP, the school board, on February 9, 1965, agreed to desegregate Guilford Elementary School in September of that year instead of waiting an additional two years. The simple mention of this in the board's minutes reads: "Following a discussion, and upon motion duly made and seconded, the Board unanimously agreed to integrate the Guilford School in 1965."[249] Prior to this decision, the board had concerns about integration of White students into the two Black schools (Tubman and Guilford), believing that it would take a period of "emotional adjustment to this part of the program on the part of both white and negro parents."[250]

Perhaps the decision to close the Tubman School was influenced by the feared lack of adjustment of older White children attending Tubman

School, or perhaps not, but the board recommended to use Tubman as an elementary school instead and to build a new high school next door to it.[251] It was eventually decided to close the Tubman School, leaving Guilford Elementary School as the only former "colored school" that became fully integrated in 1965 and is still operating in the county.[252] It is a historic property and should be recognized as such.

There is a story that has been circulated by politicians that when Dr. Edward Cochran was appointed to the school board, he cast the deciding vote to end segregation. But the vote to end segregation at Guilford Elementary School was unanimous at the expense of the closure of the Harriet Tubman School. Although it was a wonderful and dramatic story told, at least the part of it regarding the vote was incorrect.[253] In 2012, forty-seven years after HoCo schools were desegregated, the board of education of HoCo issued an "Apology for the Operation of a Racially Segregated School System."[254]

THE CHILDREN ARE WATCHING

Roger Sylvester Carter, the grandson of Willis J. Carter, grew up in Guilford and settled in Ellicott City, where his legacy stands. The Roger Carter Community Center in Ellicott City is near the old Fels Lane neighborhood, about a half a mile from where he settled. He was best known as a dedicated and kind bus driver, the first Black man who received a county bus contract to take children to and from school, and for his community service with the local Rotary Club, the HoCo Economic Development Advisory Committee, the Regional Economic Development Advisory Committee, the HoCo Planning Board, the HoCo Chamber of Commerce, the YMCA, Kiwanis, Head Start and more. He was also a loving husband, father, uncle, brother and grandfather.

Roger Carter was born on October 18, 1915, and after attending the public Guilford Elementary School, he wanted to continue his education.[255] His family said he always wanted to be a doctor, but access to education was almost impossible. The problem he faced after elementary school was that in the 1920s, there were no public high schools for Black children in HoCo. The only accessible high school for Roger was Lakeland High School in College Park, Prince Georges County.[256]

Lakeland High School was one of two high schools for Black children that opened in 1923, the other being in the southern part of Prince Georges County. Lakeland High School, like the 1923 Guilford Elementary School, was built in part using funds from the Julius Rosenwald Foundation. Carter would leave home each day at six thirty in the morning and make his way to Laurel, usually walking, to catch a bus down Route 1 to College Park, followed by a short walk to Lakeland, in time for his nine o'clock classes. He would return home and do his chores and homework just in time for bed.[257]

Carter's family were lifelong Baptists; his grandfather started the First Baptist Church of Guilford. But he fell in love with a young woman, Agnes Crawford, and to get married, Carter converted to Catholicism and moved to downtown Ellicott City, where his uncle Walter was already living and in business.[258] In 1942, he and his wife, Agnes, started an automotive repair business, and she was involved in most aspects of the business.[259] Carter's sense of community service was so strong that during a heavy rainstorm in July 1945, he volunteered to dislodge some logs, keeping a floodgate on Tiber Branch open, but he fell into the water and was swept three hundred feet downstream. Fortunately, he survived with only minor injuries, as the newspapers reported.[260]

Transportation was added to the Carters' business when a priest asked Roger whether he could transport Black children from Doughoregan Manor to the St. Paul Catholic School in Ellicott City. He did it in an old army surplus station wagon that the family called the "carry-all." In 1949, Roger and Agnes purchased their first bus through a loan, earning a HoCo bus contract to transport Black children to and from the new Harriett Tubman High School. Part of their county payment was sent directly to the bank to pay for the bus. Agnes was their first bus driver and managed the business side of things, while Roger repaired vehicles, kept the bus running and solicited new business.[261]

It didn't take long for Roger and Agnes's bus service, formally known as the Carter Bus Service Inc., to grow and take on more community activities. After the schools were fully desegregated in 1965, Carter buses continued to take children back and forth to their schools and events. The company also had a public service contract for weekend trips to correctional facilities as far away as Hagerstown, for which Roger himself was the driver.[262]

Roger and Agnes also had an interest in history. Agnes had been a student in the Ellicott City Colored School, and when it was for sale in 1973, they purchased the property from the church that owned it.[263] In the mid-1970s, Roger teamed up with Roger Marino to form R&R Tour Lines Ltd. to conduct "Ellicott City Howard County Historical Tours." An advertisement from 1977 described "essentially a tour of Ellicott City, Elkridge, and parts of the eastern area of the county—including old brick

Roger Carter (*left*). *Courtesy of Joan Carter-Smith.*

church, Thomas Viaduct, Lawyers Hill, Ilchester, mill area of Ellicott City, Patapsco Institute." The contact in the ad was Joetta Koppenhoefer, also known as Joetta Cramm, a popular local historian.[264]

Roger and Agnes intended to feature the Ellicott City Colored School in their history tours and to do more with the building, but they never had the time. Roger died in 1984, and Agnes finally sold her childhood school building to HoCo in 1995.[265]

Many folks still remember the friendly bus service from their childhoods. The Carter Bus Company would often charter its bus for youth events, charging only for the time of the driver, and in the 1980s, Roger and Agnes also transported children to the county's Head Start centers. When Roger died in 1984, Agnes took over the day-to-day operations of the company and its twelve buses. When Agnes retired, their daughter Sylvia took over the business. Sylvia, her daughter Wanda and other family members all filled in as bus drivers at one time or another.[266] Sylvia was also a trailblazer, becoming the first woman in HoCo in the Ellicott City Rotary.[267]

One of Roger Carter's legacies is ensuring his family took personal responsibility, had a strong work ethic and preferred entrepreneurship. Throughout all of this was living an honorable life, because, as his granddaughter Wanda emphasized, "the children are watching," and adults should live their lives "so that children who see you will know what a decent, responsible adult looks like."[268] The Roger Carter Center unveiled a portrait of its namesake this year for an emotional crowd, with speeches by the county executive and family members Wanda Wilson Garcia and Joan Carter-Smith.[269] Let's all remember: the children are watching.

Chapter 8

GUILFORD'S HEYDAY

For the past one hundred years, Guilford has been a relatively quiet community most notable for its churches, its schools and surviving the Columbia development. But for the two decades before that, Guilford was one of the centers of excitement and business in HoCo, primarily due to the establishment of the Maryland Granite Company and the Patuxent Branch rail line that the company brought, connecting to Savage.

MARYLAND GRANITE COMPANY

Leading up to Guilford's heyday was a granite quarry business boom that started in the late 1890s and early 1900s when the Guilford Granite, Howard Granite, Guilford and Waltersville Granite and Maryland Granite Companies began operations. By far the biggest and most prosperous of the companies was the Maryland Granite Company, which finally brought the B&O Railroad to Guilford.

In 1900, the *Baltimore Sun* made an announcement of a B&O Railroad extension planned from Savage to Guilford, "intended to afford transportation facilities for the large and important granite quarries at Guilford, the product of which is exceedingly valuable."[270] The Guilford Quarry Railroad was completed quickly and opened in April 1901.[271]

When the Maryland Granite Company began operating in 1901, it was to be the most modern quarry operation possible. The company would own and operate its railway siding, telegraph and telephone service, post office and company store, as well as housing for its workers.[272] There would also be a new community hall and a large hotel for up to two hundred workers.[273] A machine and blacksmith shop were needed to maintain the large steam plant and air compressor to operate power hoists, drills and pneumatic tools and a three-motor-type twenty-ton overhead traveling crane in addition to the cutting shop, polishing machines and all the latest appliances for cutting and dressing granite.[274]

The description by *Monumental News* in 1902 of these operations is impressive:

> *The cutting shed is 400 feet long by 60 feet wide, with two travelling cranes. There are two 150 horsepower boilers and engines. Thirty-five compressed air hand tools and several surfacing machines are in use and others are to be added. Eighteen hundred cubic feet of free air is generated a minute, compressed air being used to operate the derricks and drills on the quarries as well as the surfacing and hand tools in the shed. There are seven derricks. Two new ones now being put up have Oregon pine masts 100 feet long, 28 inches at the butt and 25 inches at the top. They are being equipped with Whitcomb Brothers' latest improved hoists and turning gear. The booms are 86 feet long. Twenty new cottages and a boarding house are being built and land has been deeded by the company for a schoolhouse and church. When fully in operation 400 work men will be employed, of which about one-half will be stone cutters.*[275]

In 1908, the United States Geological Survey (USGS) noted:

> *The Maryland Granite Company's quarry is on the east side of Little Patuxent River 2 miles north of Savage Factory and about 5 miles northwest of Annapolis Junction. It is the principal quarry in the Guilford area and was the only one operating at the time of examination in 1908.... The quarry measures about 500 by 300 feet and has a depth of about 100 feet. The average depth of stripping is about 10 feet. The sheets, 3 to 10 feet thick, are approximately horizontal and tapering lenticular. Vertical joints strike north-south and east-west, recurring at wide intervals.*[276]

Maryland Granite Company marked the industry pinnacle for Guilford and employed hundreds of workers, many of whom molded the modern town of Guilford. In 1901, Reverend Willis Carter, a minister and skilled granite

MARYLAND GRANITE COMPANY

New Corporation Formed For Operating The Guilford Quarries.

A charter for the incorporation of the Maryland Granite Company of Baltimore has just been filed, with a capital stock of $100,000, that will be increased at once to $200,000 by the issue of $100,000 preferred stock.

The incorporators of the new company are: W. T. Stilwell, president of the Structural Iron and Steel Company; William H. Evans, president Evans Marble Company; John Howard Herrick, stone dealer, Baltimore city; George R. Gaither, attorney, and Frederick Snare, president Snare & Triest Engineering Company, of New York city.

The company recently purchased the Gault granite quarries, located at Guilford, Howard county, in this State, together with what is known as the Gary Cotton Mills property, including its water rights on the Patuxent river, and the adjoining Lohman farm and Earp quarry properties, aggregating in all about 200 acres.

The contract has been let for the building of a standard gauge railway from Savage Mills to these quarries, which will give the new granite company direct railway facilities for the shipment of its granite. Contracts have also been let for hoisting engines, traveling cranes, power derricks, compressed air drills, steam engines, boilers, railway sidings, water power equipment and for such additional machinery and fixtures as will properly equip the quarries.

Article about the new Maryland Granite Company, 1901. *From the* Evening Times *(Washington, D.C.).*

driller from Richmond, Virginia, had only recently arrived in Guilford to work in those quarries. Reverend Carter worked in the Guilford quarries, as did Jacob Coleman, George Green, Richard Chaney, Dennis Harding, Maurice Thomas, Richard Carter (son of Reverend Carter), Ed Warner, Raymond Brown, Wade Watkins, Joseph William, Albert Moore, Henry Boston and so many others. Some of these workers represent the founding families of the First Baptist Church of Guilford started by Reverend Carter in 1900/1901.[277]

William H. Evans, the president and owner of the company, died in January 1917. On July 18, 1917, the plant and equipment "formerly the property of Maryland Granite Company at Guilford, Howard County, MD" was advertised for auction, including "all the modern machinery, railroad rails" amounting to about a mile weighing between 125 and 150 tons, engines, boilers, derricks and much more.[278] This sale of equipment from the quarry should dispel the myth that it shut down due to being flooded. By 1919, the remarkable story of the Maryland Granite Company ended in the dissolution of the company. This also marked the end of the Guilford quarry industry after eighty-five years of operation by a variety of workers and companies.

THE CARTER FAMILY

A lasting gift the Maryland Granite Company gave the community was hiring a Black quarry worker by the name of Willis J. Carter. Carter was born in 1858 to Albert and Louisa Fleming Carter in Richmond, Virginia. Like his parents, Carter was enslaved until the end of the Civil War. His father Albert's occupation was shoemaker, as listed in the 1872 Freedman

Bank records, which also included the names of each family member.[279] This was confirmed in his 1899 obituary, as follows:

> *Just before the war the family that his wife belonged to brought her and the children to Richmond and in order to be near her, Mr. Carter hired himself and came to this city also; and worked at his trade—that of a shoemaker—which he learned at night while a slave. He made shoes for the Confederate Government, thus escaping much of the outside hardships of life.*[280]

Carter, at twenty-two, was listed as a shoemaker in the 1880 census, as was his father in 1872 and his oldest brother, William. His older brother, Albert J., listed as twenty-nine, was a quarryman, as was a twenty-year-old neighbor. Quarry work in the Richmond area seemed to be a good trade, with the many granite quarries in the area. Albert Jr. and Carter appear to have been the first in their family to read and write.[281]

Census forms are all but absent for 1890 due to a fire at the National Archives in St. Louis, but in the 1891 Richmond directory, Carter was listed as a block cutter, a skilled career he would continue.[282] His brother Joshua died of a stroke at only twenty-three years old in 1895, and Carter attended his funeral before returning to Baltimore "where he engineers a large work."[283]

Carter was probably living in Granite, Maryland, as a quarry worker when he attended his brother's funeral. The Guilford and Waltersville Granite Company was the main employer in the area. He had temporarily left his wife and family behind in Richmond to seek a better opportunity in Maryland. While he was gone, Mary was busy raising their children while she managed a farm in the upper part of Henrico County as well as a garden and small farm at her home.[284]

Carter and his wife were located in Granite, Baltimore County, where their son Charles was born in August 1896.[285] Carter sold his property in Henrico County, Virginia, in November 1897.[286] Sadly, his older brother Albert Jr. died in an accident just two months after their father passed away.[287] Carter was still living in Granite, Maryland, in June 1900, working as a skilled driller in that quarry.[288]

As early as 1900, Carter was the first pastor of the First Baptist Church of Guilford, which he ran out of his rented house.[289] Carter, his brother James (a block cutter in the quarry) and three others obtained one acre of land property in October 1903 from Henry A. Penny Jr. for a church

Left: Reverend Willis Carter. *Courtesy First Baptist Church of Guilford.*

Below: The original First Baptist Church of Guilford. *1971 Church Bulletin.*

building, and three months later, Penny sold Willis and Mary about fourteen acres of land for their own home and farm, which employed many in the community.[290]

Mary Carter began a small school at the church, and in 1905, the board of education provided a public school teacher for their school. Among the first named trustees of this new school was Willis Carter. Carter family members supported the public schools for the next seventy years.[291]

Reverend Carter died in 1906 at just forty-nine years of age from abdominal cancer. Quarry work and stonecutting were occupations associated with this disease due to exposure from the mineral dusts.[292] After his death, Mary continued the farm and was viewed as the mother of the church due to her dedication to the church, her family and the Guilford community.

The Reverend Carter's family left quite a legacy. His oldest son, Richard, worked on the family farm but also as a quarry worker and entrepreneur whose businesses included a grocery store, an auto repair shop and a gas station. Richard's wife, Dora Mack Carter, helped with these businesses and ran the grocery store for several decades. She also taught music at the church and ran the Sunday school for over fifty years. The store across from the Guilford Elementary School was demolished in favor of new homes in 2022.[293]

Carter's second oldest son, Samuel, helped his mother run the farm and also helped build the Guilford Elementary School in 1923 with William Arthur.[294] Samuel's son, Roger, opened an auto repair shop in Ellicott City. Roger also filled a critical need for the Black community in Guilford before school integration by opening a bus company that operated for over forty years.

Carter's other children included Junius, who served overseas in World War I; Walter, who was the first Black taxi cab owner in HoCo and ran a food and drink establishment in Ellicott City; and Frank, who died in 1918 at sixteen when a train hit the vehicle his brother Walter was driving.[295] Charles served in World War I and is interred in Baltimore National Cemetery.[296] His daughter Ida died when she was an infant.[297]

Generations of the Carter family, including their spouses, have honorably served their county and have been entrepreneurs, activists and so much more to make Guilford and HoCo the communities they are today. The patriarch of the Carter family, and of modern Guilford, was clearly Reverend Willis J. Carter. His legacy continues.

Guilford Day

The first Guilford Day occurred in the summer of 1906 during the heyday of the quarries. The annual August festival continued until 1920, representing fifteen annual summer celebrations during the time of the Maryland Granite Company's success and the B&O Patuxent Branch railroad bringing visitors to Guilford from all over the region.

Headlines from the first Guilford Day, held on August 30, 1906, read, "Everybody Pleased," "The Guilford Day Celebration a Big Success," "Penny's Park in Future Will Be the Mecca for the Sixth District When People Want a Place for Public Entertainments or Outdoor Meetings." A game of baseball between the Savage and Scaggsville teams was featured, with Scaggsville winning 4–2. After the baseball game, "the Scotchmen took the adjoining field for their football game" featuring teams of married men versus bachelors. Finally came the grand tournament with "seventeen knights in the professional class and nineteen knights for the amateur class." Lest we forget, the winner of the best-looking baby contest was Isabelle Holtman Renelli of Ellicott City.[298]

These celebrations became the biggest in the region, and the following year, in 1907, they were attended by the top politicians of the era, such as Baltimore's Mayor Mahool and Maryland state senator Gorman Jr. (the son of recently deceased U.S. Senator Gorman) with 3,500 attendees.[299] In addition to the picnic, first hosted by local farmer Henry A. Penny in Penny's Grove, the main event was tilting, a form of jousting, but baseball competitions were also popular.

Attendance at this annual event reached six thousand in 1910, when it was held in Dorsey's Grove.[300] The picnic and tournaments continued each year, attracting the politicians and prominent citizens of the area, and the location was shifted to near the "Old Brick Church," which was also known as the Christ Church of Guilford and is located off Oakland Mills and Dobbin Road.

The twelfth annual event in 1917, the year that the Maryland Granite Company closed, drew three thousand participants, and there were two thousand each in the following two years.[301] The final event, on Saturday, August 14, 1920, was advertised as "The Great Guilford Day Tournament—Bigger, Brighter, and More Attractive Than Ever." This fifteenth and final annual event was one of the two main picnics in the county that everyone looked forward to attending. It was reported to be a success, but folks didn't know it would be the last one.[302] In 1921, the

Left: Guilford Day ad, 1904. *From the* Ellicott City Times.

Right: Mayor Mahool at 1907 Guilford Day. *From the* Baltimore Sun.

Guilford Day Association was listed as tax delinquent following the demise of the quarry industry in Guilford.[303] Picnics at Guilford still occurred, but these affairs were nothing compared to Guilford Day during its heyday.

1920s MURDER MYSTERY

James Bernard Pattison was a likeable and happy man in his thirties. He was known to be sociable and was in fact reported to be "harmless and usually went about singing," but many felt he had a slight mental affliction. He visited many of his neighbors, including Ross Pease and his wife, Marbelle

Pease, many times.[304] His brother Thomas was concerned that he wasn't holding down a steady job and filed a police warrant for vagrancy. Thomas didn't know his brother had already found employment at another nearby farm owned by James Oursler. Sometimes, between jobs, he wandered off for several days at a time, so when he didn't show for work, Oursler wasn't immediately concerned. Part of Thomas's concern for his brother's stability was that Pattison had some minor mental health issues and had spent several months in the Springfield Asylum near Sykesville before being recently released as "cured." Pattison was last seen walking on his brother's property in the evening of May 11.[305]

While walking through the sprawling woods on Thursday, May 18, along the property of Thomas Pattison, neighbor William Carr and his son Henry discovered a body—a badly decomposed body, at that. The authorities had few clues but were able to identify the dead man by the initials on his underwear—it was James Bernard Pattison. He had by then been reported missing. Neighbors reported hearing two gunshots the night Pattison went missing but paying no attention, since this was not an uncommon event, probably due to the hundred-plus acres of land being used for target practice, hunting or just shooting for fun.[306]

But how did J. Bernard Pattison die? A coroner's jury was convened, and the jurors' first thought was that Pattison committed suicide, but there was no gun found at the scene, and he had two bullet wounds to his head. That pointed to murder. His death certificate listed the cause as a "pistol shot into right side of brain," concluding: "homicide-murder." But the jury was not able to identify any suspects and determined Pattison was killed by unknown persons. Detective James Manning from the Baltimore Police Department was then assigned to the case at the request of the state's attorney, Clark.[307]

Held On Murder Charge

WILLIAM CARTER CRONMILLER AND MRS. MARY BELLE PEASE

Mrs. Pease and Cronmiller are charged with the murder of J. Bernard Pattison, who was shot to death in a strip of woods in Howard county several months ago. They were photographed today by the bureau of identification of the Baltimore Police Department and tonight they will be taken back to Ellicott City to await trial.

Mug shots of Cronmiller and Pease, 1922. *From the* Evening Sun.

Without a murder weapon or suspect, the investigation was stalled, so Pattison's brother-in-law hired his own private detective to assist. We aren't sure how the police initially figured out that Marbelle

Pease was involved, but on August 5, they arrested both her and an uncle. It was reported that the uncle was not a true suspect and was only arrested to pressure Pease into providing more information, and it worked! She ended up confessing that William Carter Cronmiller killed Pattison, and she and her uncle were then released.[308] But Cronmiller wasn't going to take the fall for it.

On August 7, 1922, the *Baltimore Sun* reported that Guilford residents Cronmiller, twenty-nine, and Pease, twenty-seven, were charged with the murder of James Bernard Pattison. Cronmiller and Pease were lovers, and while Pease was separated from her husband, allegedly due to their affair, a divorce was never filed. Cronmiller's wife, Carrie, was granted a divorce just two years earlier on charges her husband committed adultery. If the affair between Pease and Cronmiller had been going on for five years, as claimed, she may have been the reason for Cronmiller's divorce.[309]

Pattison became aware of their affair when, during one of his visits with Pease, she told him of the secret meetings she had with Cronmiller, and at one point he allegedly threatened to tell her husband, Ross Pease. That provided a motive, and when arrested, Pease and Cronmiller each accused the other of murdering Pattison.[310] On September 15, during a court appearance, they both pled not guilty and requested to be tried separately. The trial was moved to Anne Arundel County.[311]

Under oath, Pease recounted an odd event that occurred involving her and Pattison. The previous November, Pattison visited Pease outside

GUN LOCATED IN GUILFORD QUARRY

Weapon Which Caused Death Of J. B. Pattison Identified. Officials Gathering Evidence.

The revolver with which J. Bernard Pattison was shot and killed last May was found in the old quarry in Guilford last Sunday. It was found almost exactly at the point which Mrs. Pease had told the authorities it had been thrown. Much trouble was experienced by officials in pumping the water out of the huge reservoir. It was estimated by experts that in this hole there was probably 1,250,000 gallons of water. The pumping apparatus went out of commission several times and on Sunday when about a foot of water had been pumped that day Deputy Frank Miller found the gun sticking muzzle down in the mud. There was still from seven to ten feet of water in the quarry. The gun was identified by Benjamin Somers as having been sold by him on April 1st last to W. C. Cronmiller, who is being held for the action of the grand jury charged with implication in Pattison's death.

Mr. Somers said that Cronmiller had entered his store on April 1 and asked for a gun. When he showed him one Cronmiller wanted to know whether it was any good. Mr. Somers told him to try it for a few days and if he did not want it to bring it back and, if it proved satisfactory to pay him for it. On April 8th Mr. Somers was paid for the gun. It is a 38 calibre.

Gun located in Guilford Quarry, 1922.
From the Ellicott City Times.

her home, carrying a shotgun. She said he "riddled the clothes on the clothesline," after which he claimed he "only shot to scare" her. Holding a revolver she had borrowed from a neighbor, she said, "Well, I'll shoot to scare you," and she fired the gun twice at him, resulting in Pattison dropping the shotgun and running off. It is reported that shortly after this incident, he went to the Springfield Asylum.[312]

Though Pattison was killed on May 11, it wasn't until August 4 that Cronmiller and Pease were arrested for the killing. She accused him of the murder and of then giving her the gun he used when they met up later. She admitted to throwing the murder weapon into a quarry near the property. The quarry containing the gun was the old Guilford and Waltersville quarry just east of the Little Patuxent River off the dirt pathway. The .27-caliber gun was eventually found after draining over a million gallons of water from the more-than-thirty-foot hole. The gun was identified by Benjamin Somers, an Ellicott City merchant, as the one he sold to Cronmiller.[313]

During their confinement in the Ellicott City Jail awaiting trial, Cronmiller paid a trustee working in the prison to deliver six love letters to Pease. However, the letters were given to the warden instead and would eventually sway the jury tremendously. One of the letters, printed by the *Baltimore American*, read:

> *Sweetheart: Why don't you answer or write me a line? Gee, but I hate to see you in here, and I also hate to be here myself, but I can't say a word, only why did you let them pick anything out of you?*
>
> *Say, darling, who is coming to see you tomorrow? Are you expecting anyone? What is Ross Pease saying about this? I guess he is giving me Hell, ain't he? Say, what do you think we will get; about 10 or 20 years, that is, if we don't get a good lawyer, but I am going to fight it to a finish, and I want you to do the same. But don't care, and I won't put it on you. I am awful sorry that I said what I did, but you put it on me so strong I got mad and said anything, for, if I had not said a word, they would not have had as much to work on.*
>
> *Well, darling, cheer up; we will make the best of it, and when everything is over I want you and only you, so, if it is 20 years, will you be true to me? Well, darling, I would like to be with you tonight. Well, I guess I will stop for tonight. With lots of love. Answer at once if not sooner. Write on back of this, please.*[314]

During the police investigation, Cronmiller and Pease each accused the other of the murder and disposing of the gun in the quarry. The murder trial began on October 23 with Cronmiller's mother testifying that her son told her the evening of the murder that Pease killed Pattison and she got rid of the gun. Pease testified against Cronmiller, but it seemed the letters influenced the jury's decision. He wasn't the only one who wrote love letters. In fact, when the defense read aloud letters she allegedly wrote, Pease admitted in court that she had written several letters to Cronmiller while they were in jail, including one asking for money. The court did not feel those letters were significant.[315]

On October 26, Cronmiller was convicted of second-degree murder. He was sentenced to eighteen years in prison. Pease would be tried separately. When Cronmiller was offered the opportunity to speak before the sentencing, he stated, "Your Honor, I am the victim of a woman's false statements." After the conviction, the HoCo state's attorney added, "Cronmiller and Pease were the only persons who had any real knowledge of the murder…and this information had to be dragged from them inch by inch."[316]

Pease was quickly put on trial in November 1922. There was difficulty getting a jury since so many prospective members said they had already formed an opinion on her guilt or innocence. The court ended up finding jurors from Anne Arundel County, of which nine found for acquittal and three felt Pease was guilty.[317] A new trial was scheduled in Annapolis for November 10, and Pease was released after providing bail. Ironically, Ross Pease, her husband and a quarry worker, provided the bail and took her home, as they were reported to have reconciled.[318] Pease was apparently never tried again. After Ross's death, Marbelle moved to North Carolina, remarried in 1959 and died in Florida in 1989 at age eighty-eight.[319]

While in the Baltimore penitentiary, Cronmiller was listed as a machinist in an iron foundry.[320] He applied for and was granted parole in 1930. In August 1932, he was "pardoned to restore citizenship" by Maryland governor Albert Ritchie based on a recommendation from the parole commissioner and "reputable citizens of the State."[321] He married again and had three more children while living on Ninth Street in Laurel. Cronmiller worked for the U.S. government in the Washington Navy Yard after his pardon through the early 1940s.[322] He died in 1945 and is buried in Ivy Hill Cemetery in Laurel with his second wife.[323]

RITCHIE APPROVES 35 PAROLES, PARDON

Raymond M. Hilton, Sentenced To Two Years For Bigamy, Considered

AUTO THIEF, 18, ON LIST

Several Negroes Are Among Cases Considered By Governor Ritchie

Thirty-five paroles and a pardon have been approved by Governor Ritchie and will become effective August 1 unless objections are presented.

judge advises that he thought at the time of trial that the proper sentence was three years with a parole after six months, if the man's prison conduct justified it, and that he advised Thal's attorney that he would recommend a parole on the expiration of six months. The man's prison conduct has been good, and inasmuch as he has served the sentence which the judge intended him to serve I will grant him a parole.

Sentenced To 18 Years

WILLIAM CARTER CRONMILLER—Sentenced by the Circuit Court for Anne Arundel County to eighteen years in the Penitentiary for second-degree murder. About seven years and three months of his term remain. Cronmiller and the man he killed appear to have been infatuated with the same woman. She turned out to be a bad actor and she and Cronmiller were both indicted for murder. After the man's conviction the woman was tried, but the jury disagreed and her case has not been brought up since. Cronmiller lived in Howard county and a great many reputable citizens of his community feel that he should be released, one of them being the brother of the man he killed. He had been a good and industrious citizen before his offense and has been an excellent prisoner, I think he is entitled to another chance.

Governor Ritchie approves William Cronmiller's parole, 1930. *From the* Baltimore Sun.

It was striking and sad to see this message left on Cronmiller's Find a Grave page from his great-granddaughter, who was under the mistaken impression that he had killed a woman's husband:

> *Great grandpa, what did you do?*
> *You must have really loved that woman*
> *to kill her husband. RIP.* [324]

If only she knew the truth: her great-grandfather was pardoned after serving ten years in the penitentiary in Baltimore. Things we do in life can certainly have unexpected consequences.

So, who done it? It still could have been Cronmiller, as the jury decided. But Pease could have killed James Bernard Pattison so her husband wouldn't find out about her affair with Cronmiller, and Cronmiller could have helped her cover up the crime. Since she had the murder weapon, she likely threw the gun in the quarry and had more motive than Cronmiller, who was later pardoned for the crime. She had shot a revolver at Pattison once before when he messed up her clothesline with a shotgun, and she had told him about her affair with Cronmiller. What do you think? We will never know for sure. Regardless, Pattison certainly didn't deserve this fate.

Chapter 9

OUR SAVAGE NEIGHBORS

BEGINNING OF SAVAGE MILL

Two HoCo mill towns each celebrated a significant anniversary in 2022—Ellicott City and Savage. In Ellicott City, the EC250 celebration commemorated the arrival of the Ellicott brothers in 1772, and Savage celebrated the one-hundredth anniversary of the dedication of Carroll Baldwin Hall.[325] Savage Mill stuck with its self-proclaimed anniversary date of 1816, which is not supported by research. Where did this 1816 date come from?

The land on which the mills sit was not in the possession of John Savage or the Williams brothers until after 1822.[326] So why did folks decide to celebrate 1816 as their anniversary? According to Filby, renovation in the 1940s uncovered on a window frame the blue-pencil inscription, "Ted Sullivan, April 16, 1816." Filby did not claim this was an actual date of a building's construction, but it has created a legend repeated often in the folklore of Savage.[327] No one knows who Ted Sullivan was or if the date was a birthdate or another date. It also seems extremely unlikely that blue pencils were around during those days, although it was in the later 1800s.

Researching history can be confusing at times—well, much of the time. When examining the chancery court case of *Amos Williams versus SMC*, December 1821 was the date provided more than once for when the company was incorporated.[328] December 1821 was when the incorporation bill was submitted to the Maryland General Assembly in its

1821 legislative session, and an index for the 1821 session lists that year for the incorporation of SMC.[329]

Making it confusing is the February 22, 1822 date, which is when the bill was legally approved by both houses of the general assembly. So the Savage community could select either December 1821 or February 22, 1822, to be used as an anniversary date, but they chose neither, apparently sticking to the mythical anniversary of 1816. But could the Williams brothers have started building a mill earlier than 1822? We see no evidence of that, especially since they didn't own the land.

SMC purchased over 200 acres of land within a year of its incorporation and began building its factory immediately. In April 1822, SMC purchased 50 acres of Pinkstones Thicket, which was "east of the falls of patuxent [sic] River and a small way below the Island of the river," as well as 114¼ acres of Warfield's Range on the west side of the river extending to Hammond's Branch, to expand its holdings for future expansion of the "factory."[330]

In July, SMC purchased 87¼ acres of Venison Park and Brothers Partnership on the south side of the Little Patuxent river adjoining the Warfield's Range parcel, extending to "what is called the great Falls on said river."[331] The next large land purchases were in January 1823, when Gideon White sold to John Savage the tracts known as Mill Land (8½ acres) and Whites Contrivance (200 acres), and then, in March 1823, SMC took out a $20,000 mortgage from John Savage on the land it had already purchased in 1822.[332] The mortgage stated there were "fixtures and machinery in and about the factory erected by the Savage Manufacturing Company…upon a tract of land called White's Contrivance," which was purchased in January 1823.[333]

Back in those days, when you had property, you could build quickly if you had the funds. And the Williams brothers, thanks to John Savage and others, had the funds.

BECOMING SAVAGE FACTORY

By 1824, the Savage cotton mill had one thousand spindles operating, with a capacity of five thousand; 120 power looms; and two hundred workers employed.[334] By the 1830s, SMC ran the following enterprises, making its operation a factory: cotton mill, gristmill, sawmill, foundry, machine shop, furnace, bleaching works, wheelwright shop and railroad.[335]

Amos Williams, the on-site agent for the company, planned on adding another cotton mill and more works to the mix. To accommodate the

THE SAVAGE MANUFACTURING COMPANY'S COTTON MILL AND WORKS FOR SALE.—The business pursuits of the present shareholders of the above company being inconsistent with manufacturing operations of any kind, they will offer at public sale, at the Exchange, in this city, on THURSDAY, the 8th of October next, at one o'clock P. M., ALL THEIR WORKS ON THE PATUXENT RIVER, in Howard county, and binding on the Washington turnpike, 16 miles from the city of Baltimore. The works consist of

A large COTTON MILL, of 140 looms and 4,500 spindles, well equipped, with machinery in good order, and to which, at a small cost, a few recent modern improvements could be added. A large sized MACHINE SHOP, a CUPOLA FURNACE, BLACKSMITH'S and WHEELWRIGHT SHOPS, GRIST MILL, a LARGE COUNTRY STORE, MANAGER'S HOUSE, with from seventy to eighty tenements for operatives, mostly brick, together with Two Hundred and Seventy-three Acres of LAND. The water power and works are so well known, and as purchasers will examine for themselves, all further description of them is unnecessary.

There will also be sold, with or without the above, a WATER POWER, below on the same stream, of twelve feet eight inches, with about eighty acres of Land attached thereto, which may be connected or improved separately by a paper or grist mill, for which its site and locality are well adapted.

The above property lies about a mile from the Washington Branch Railroad, with which it can be connected by a short railroad, for which the grading is already made.

Persons wishing to view the property, by application at the office of the Company, No. 30 South Frederick street, will be provided with every convenience therefor by conveyance to and from the railroad on the same day.

The charter, which is perpetual, and authorizes any species of manufacturing, will be sold with the property if desired.

The TOOLS of the machine shop and foundery PATTERNS will be sold on the premises on THURSDAY, Oct. 15, at 12 o'clock M., whether the factory be sold or not.

Terms of sale for the works, &c.:—One-fourth cash; one-fourth in twelve months, and the balance, if properly secured and if desired, in five years, with interest payable semi-annually.

GIBSON & CO.,
a20 2aw&ds†   Auctioneers.

SMC for sale in 1857. *From the Baltimore Sun.*

waterpower to run the operations without affecting the existing factory, the company took water from Hammond Branch and the "North Branch" of the Little Patuxent to feed into the milldam.[336]

In 1850, a wheelwright shop produced 36 wagon carts and the two-person blacksmith shop used 5 tons of bar iron and 1,000 bushels of coals to make its products that year. The machine shop and foundry produced cotton-milling machinery and castings from 500 tons of bar steel using 1 cupola blast furnace. The sawmill made 70,000 feet of oak and poplar planks from 700 logs, and the gristmill made 2,650 bushels of superior wheat flour,

75,000 pounds of corn meal and 5,000 bushels of feed. The cotton mill used enormous amounts of cotton (22,000 bales), oil, starch and wood to make thousands of yards of cotton sheeting running 5,000 spindles and 140 looms employing 250 workers.[337]

With this huge factory operation, why did they need to sell it? Amos Williams was ambitious. His authority to act on business ventures and invest the company's funds became a question that was subject to a chancery court case, *Amos Williams versus SMC*, in 1848, which was eventually settled.[338] Part of the problem arose when Amos made expensive investments in the company's railroad, bridge and furnace, which put it further into debt. The cotton operation was the most profitable business, but he thought they could do better. Amos Williams formed the Savage Railroad Company, built a horse-drawn railroad from the mill to the Washington Branch line and charged SMC higher than standard rates for the shipment of goods.[339]

Unfortunately, the business fell apart when Amos Williams became quite ill and was incapacitated from his job for several years, resulting in questions about how he ran the factory. The constant investment of funds in operations other than cotton manufacturing created financial difficulties, as the foundry required an extensive wood supply and the cotton mill competed for the limited water supply for power, as did the furnace. Instead of paying down the original debt from the mortgage owed to John Savage, the continued investments were too much for SMC to overcome. The factory had to be sold to cover debts and was eventually sold to William H. Baldwin in 1859.[340]

A Real Christmas Story

For a brief time, Savage was the Christmas capital of the country, thanks to Harry Harrison Heim. Heim was born in Baltimore on March 14, 1883. He moved with his family to San Diego before World War I, where he worked as a display manager and merchant for Marston Company's Department Store, even winning several awards for his merchandise displays.[341] In about 1936, he began to create Christmas ornaments in San Diego, especially in the form of blown glass balls.[342]

By 1940, Heim was back in Baltimore, and in 1941, he established Santa Novelties Inc.[343] Heim was expanding his business quickly, and in 1944, he made twelve million Christmas tree balls in his Baltimore factory on East Lombard Street, of which eleven million were made by hand.[344] The 1948 announcement that Harry Heim and Santa Novelties had bought almost five hundred acres of SMC lands was a relief "to the 1,400 residents of the Howard county town who have felt the grip of the economic depression since the mill suspended cotton operations last August."[345]

The deed between Heim's company, Santa Novelties Inc., and SMC is dated August 24, 1948. The sale price was reported to be $450,000, of which $200,000 was in mortgages to the SMC. It was reported that Heim had a $2,500,000 business, and he put everything he owned—and didn't—into his Santa Heim venture.[346]

One of the first things Heim did on his arrival in Savage was relocate his factory from Baltimore and finally fix the local housing he bought, some of which was without indoor toilets or electricity. He also broke the "paternalistic" pattern of company-owned housing, although SMC did provide low rents. He began to offer the Savage community the opportunity to purchase their homes or to continue renting fixed-up housing without the deep discount provided by SMC.[347] He was welcomed by the community even when he tried to turn Savage into "Santa Heim" in 1948 and 1949, but the novelty of a Santa village didn't last.

The Christmas of 1948 was a memorable and remarkable one. It was like a circus came into town to stay, and on opening day, five thousand children out of a total of fifteen thousand people attended, with special trains for the

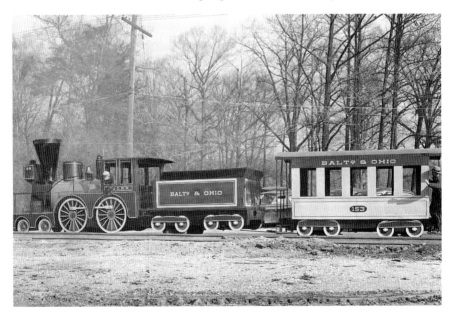

Children's ride on a Tom Thumb replica, 1948. *From the* Baltimore Sun.

attraction from Baltimore and Washington chartered by the B&O Railroad. There were reindeer, horses and animated animals and even a replica "Tom Thumb" B&O train for the kids to ride on. The town, including the post office, was painted in Christmas colors, and the Savage Post Office was flooded with letters to Santa from children across the country. Heim lined the streets of Savage with twenty-eight thousand lights and ten-foot candy canes, just like in the biggest cities. He had big dreams for Santa Heim, and that Christmas of 1948 made all things seem possible.[348]

The fanfare for 1949 and 1950 was much less, and by 1951, it was over. Some folks didn't want to change the name of Savage to Santa Heim, business fell off and workers lost wages, paint started to peel on houses Heim bought and tax debt brought more problems. Although this tax-related charge was hyped up in the newspapers, Heim ended up with only a one-hundred-dollar fine.[349] All in all, Heim did his best to pay the bills, but the money coming in just wasn't enough to cover expenses. He sold what he could to the National Store Fixture Company in October 1950 before the IRS put the rest up for public auction in April 1951.[350] Heim died of a heart attack less than two years later, on January 30, 1953.[351] The National Store Fixture Company owned Savage Mill until it sold its interests in 1965 to the Winer family, which still owns the mill today.[352]

HoCo's First Public Library Building

The community hall built and organized by Carroll Baldwin Memorial Institute Inc. celebrated its one-hundredth anniversary in 2022. The hall was not only a remarkable gift to the community, but it was also HoCo's first public library building. The June 23, 1922 charter for the corporation included that "the nature of the business and the objects and purposes to be transacted, are education, moral, literary and benevolent…for the exclusive benefit and advantage of the community…for a Public Library, and/or for a Community Hall."[353]

At the dedication of the hall to the community, it was described as having "a meeting room, library, kitchens, bowling alleys and a radio receiving apparatus for the pleasure of the people of the community."[354] As further indication of the importance of this new library, Rignal Baldwin was appointed to the Maryland Public Library Advisory Commission the same month.[355]

HoCo Library bookmobile, circa 1970s. *HoCo Library Board of Trustees.*

Savage was the location for a free public library as early as October 1920, sponsored by the Carroll Baldwin Memorial Library Association with support from the Maryland Public Library Commission.[356] This location would have been in the former community hall, as it seems the building of the existing Carroll Baldwin Memorial Hall did not start until May 1921.[357] In January 1922, the library moved into its new location, presumably the new hall.[358] In June 1922, SMC turned over the Carroll Baldwin Hall Memorial Library Association to the "Community Hall," which was already operating a public library along with a bowling alley.[359] This public library was still operating in 1927, with Eloise M. Oliver as librarian.[360]

The Maryland Public Library Commission visited several locations in HoCo in 1912 and reported community interest in libraries for Ellicott City and Elkridge. In fact, the commission stated that a library in Elkridge was opened on May 14, 1913, in the residence of Lina T. Stintz, the librarian.[361] The Elkridge and Savage libraries were the only two HoCo libraries reported operating in 1921–22, and Stintz and a Ms. Oliver as the librarians, respectively.[362] The Savage library was the only one operating in a public building. For the 1924–25 fiscal year, a library in Ellicott City was listed as operating since 1922 and in Savage since 1920, neither of which used public funds but both of which were free to the public.

On February 29, 1956, the Carroll Baldwin Memorial Institute became the tenth "library station" of the HoCo Public Library system.[363] It is unknown at this time how long the community hall was a library station, but there was desire to make it a branch within the county library system as the growth of the area became inevitable. In July 1966, a three-year lease was signed, with an option for three more years, for the Carroll Baldwin Memorial Library Branch, and the library opened in September as part of the county system.[364]

Book circulation was low, and this location eventually became a reading center in the 1970s.[365] But there were still big plans for a library location in Savage. In the 1980s, there was a plan for a new library and community center, and one of the suggested locations would have been part of the Patuxent Valley–Bollman Bridge school area off Vollmerhausen Road.[366] Apparently the school system did not have enough space to also include a library on the property, and the eventual location for the new library was chosen in 1991, where it currently sits, off Gorman and Knights Bridge Roads. In 2014, the library was enlarged and renovated, becoming a STEM center.[367] Carroll Baldwin Memorial Hall played a long and important role in the HoCo public library system, leading to Savage having one of the county's six successful library branches today.

Once Upon a Sundown Town

Savage was a fully segregated unincorporated town until, perhaps, the Civil Rights Movement in the 1960s.[368] Then, Black citizens were finally allowed a limited daytime presence and expected to never appear after sundown in Savage, in keeping with the image of a "sundown town."[369] Perhaps it was Savage's relative geographic isolation that contributed to it becoming as segregated as it did, but it was also a microcosm of the racism that existed throughout HoCo. In 1986, Alice Cornelison wrote that:

In any given unabridged dictionary, a savage, noun, is most likely to be defined as "a person of extreme, unfeeling, brutal cruelty." Take this person and clone the extreme, unfeeling, brutal cruelty into every brain, nerve, heart, skin, intestine, and bone cell—indeed, into every cell in the body of each white man, woman and child living in Savage, and one will have the description of the place and its inhabitants as repeated by blacks in every community of the county. Savage residents hated black people and they made certain that every black person who dared cross the unincorporated boundaries of Savage knew about it.[370]

Savage was a company mill town for Whites only. There are no written records indicating that a deliberate decision was made to segregate at the beginning of the company or as it grew. Available census records from 1850 to 1880 indicate that only fourteen Black people lived in the census area of Savage, and they were all young and part of White households. In 1870, two Black persons, both eleven-year-old female domestic servants, lived in Savage. Harriet Watkins lived in the household of the customs house officer, Samuel Mainster, and Augusta Boston lived with Samuel Isaacs, a miller, and his family.[371] The period between 1880 and 1940 recorded no Black people living in Savage.[372]

Looking at the racial demographics for the past 170 years, it is clear that Savage was a White village until about 1970. Any Black residents recorded earlier may have been an artifact of including a wider geographic area of the area than just Savage. We won't know for sure until we can see the census block data for those census years. In the 1970s and 1980s, we know that apartment and townhome rental properties opened, allowing a more economically and racially diverse population. In fact, preliminary data for 2020 from justicemap.org suggests that the White population in Savage is down to 41.6 percent compared with its sundown days.[373]

Black families have been living around the perimeter of Savage since at least 1850, especially in Asbury, Jessup and Guilford, which were within walking distance. It is not known exactly when Savage became a sundown town, but the degree of racism in Savage in the 1920s and 1930s was illustrated by two deeds that the HoCo school board obtained from SMC, owned and operated by the Baldwin family. Both deeds were written after the 1918 death of Carroll Baldwin, the longtime supervisor of Savage Mill.

On October 2, 1921, SMC sold land to the board of education for a school in Savage. The deed stated: "First, that the Grantee nor its assigns or successors in title will at any time sell, lease or convey the property hereby

Advertising the Olde Time Minstrel Show in Savage, 1956. *Savage Historical Society.*

granted to persons to negro blood."[374] Then on December 20, 1937, SMC sold the county land for another school with the same restriction.[375] The segregation in Savage was something learned early in life by HoCo Black families. It did not need to be posted or advertised—it was just known.

Perhaps these racist attitudes were celebrated by the Savage community through participation in minstrel shows at the Carroll Baldwin Hall, sometimes called the Community Hall or Memorial Hall. Even before the hall was dedicated, the traveling Howard Minstrels performed in June 1922, as they had in Highland, Glenwood and Ellicott City. It was reported that the "men taking part are anxious to go to Savage as they have been told that a packed house may be looked forward to."[376] In 1956, the "Olde Time Minstrel Show" debuted, and the second annual show was held in 1957. Both shows were sponsored by the Carroll Baldwin Memorial Association, and it is not yet known if these annual shows continued. Some of the characters portrayed using blackface included "Bones," "Tambo," "Asbestos," "Rufus," "Mumbo" and "Stop 'N' Scratch It."[377] The laughs at the expense of the nearby Black community were probably just brushed off as good old fun, but they continued the complicity of negative racial behaviors by community leaders.

In 1983, the Ku Klux Klan distributed literature in Savage, and the vice president of the Savage Fire Company board of directors, also a volunteer firefighter, brought some of the literature to the fire station, resulting in an outcry from the public asking the county to condemn the actions. The firefighter claimed it was a joke, but the seven Black firefighters at Savage were "outraged," as were Black residents of Savage.[378] The fallout from the Klan literature continued throughout the year with assaults and other violence.[379] A Black couple at the River Island apartments who faced racist acts against them moved out of the area, and a Black mother and son had to move out of Howard Hills in 1985 due to racial harassment and vandalism.[380] In all of these situations, community leaders in Savage denied racism to protect the image of their town. The operator of the only grocery store in Savage said, "I don't think anybody is against the Blacks. They stay to themselves and don't bother anybody. I would rather see some of them in my store than some Whites. They stay in their place and don't get rowdy."[381]

Prominent residents in Savage boast of today's inclusive and diverse community, in contrast to the not-so-distant past. This section is only a reminder of what some of our community members went through to foster a better understanding of some of today's social issues. Historic Savage now rivals historic Ellicott City in its inclusivity and diversity, but both could do much better. Today, it is the rare exception to hear of anything negative occurring in Savage. Yet over 80 percent of the homeowners in the community remain White, with the non-White population dominating the apartments surrounding the historic area of Savage.[382]

The Savage of yesteryear has little similarity to the present town, as its citizens have attempted to bring a more diverse view of its community into play. Carroll Baldwin Hall, which celebrated its one-hundredth anniversary in 2022, prepared a "Diversity, Equity, and Inclusion Statement" to reconcile its past. The document read, "We acknowledge that discriminatory and racist practices did regrettably occur within the community, and were likely reflected in the community's use of the hall." As well as: "The Savage of today is a markedly changed community, characterized by a colorful diversity of faith, race, ethnicity, genders, and other identities."[383]

This acknowledgement by the Carroll Baldwin Memorial Institute Inc. is appreciated by those of us who are aware of its history, and we look forward to when the Savage Community Association shares a similar acknowledgement. Driving through Savage is a treat, a throwback to an old mill town, but with fabulous hiking and walking trails, an updated regional park with tennis courts and ball fields and, of course, the Savage Mill. We encourage folks to visit Savage and indulge in the nostalgia by walking down the trails and past the old millrace and the milldam structures, seeing the mesmerizing "great falls," as they were once characterized, and walking through the mills to visit its shops and to take in a meal.

Chapter 10

COLUMBIA IS COMING!

HoCo was predominantly a rural farming community throughout most of its history. Businesses like quarries, gristmills and cotton mills and iron foundries didn't dent the agricultural character of the county. That all changed in the spring of 1963 when various companies made dozens of purchases of land, both small and large. These "new" companies had names like Cedar Farms, Farmingdale, Serenity Acres, Potomac Estates and Howard Estates. Even older, better-known companies like Town and Ranch Homes and Howard Co. Development Corp made some land purchases.[384] What no one knew is what all these companies had in common.

These companies fronted the "secret" land purchases that later became the planned community of Columbia, Maryland. The secret was let out in March 1963, and starting in June, these companies and others, including individual home sellers, sold or transferred their newly owned properties to the Howard Research and Development Corporation (HRD).[385] Over eighteen months, there were seventy deeds recorded under HRD, not including the agreements made, all from the fifth and sixth election districts—the prime targets of the new town.[386]

All told, HRD became the owner of about fourteen thousand acres of land, more than enough to fulfill the vision of James Rouse in creating a planned community of 100,000 residents—quite a bold adventure for the early 1960s.[387] When Rouse announced his plans in October 1963, just a few months after the land purchases, the fun began. In essence, a modern planned community was to be placed on top of a conservative, rural farming

Firm Planning To Develop 14,000 Acres In Howard

By EDWARD G. PICKETT
(Continued from Page 44)

something of a relief to some county officials.

Commissioner David W. Force, when contacted after yesterday's session with the developers, said: "We are very happy to learn that the purchaser is a reputable firm."

The Rouse firm is now developing, through Community Research and Development, Inc., what is called a self-contained community for 5,000 residents on 68 acres along Falls road which once was the Baltimore Country Club's Roland Park golf course.

Has Been Watched

It has also developed shopping centers throughout the east, including Mondawmin and Harundale in the Baltimore area.

The meeting yesterday with the Howard commissioners, requested by the developers, was attended by Mr. Rouse, his brother, Willard G. Rouse, William E. Finley and a company attorney.

Mr. Finley, a vice president of

the firm, has been in charge of the Village of Cross Keys development, the project on Falls road.

The purchase of the land by an unknown company beginning early this year has been watched with interest and a touch of apprehension by citizens of the county and planning officials.

Thomas Harris, planning director, noted the growing attention being paid the county by developers, and attributed much of it to the status of the county as one of the few remaining areas in the greater Baltimore region where sizable tracts of land are still available.

Housing developments in the county have been retarded by the lack of a public water and sewage system, but a $2,500,000 program for development of such a system is now under way, having begun during the summer.

Boom Expected

Construction of the system is expected to herald a vast building boom in the county.

Future plans now call for the water and sewage facilities to follow along U.S. Route 29, at a later date.

At present, not even Ellicott City has a public sewage system.

The Howard County Planning Commission noted earlier this year that "more and better housing for all economic groups" is needed in the county.

A $3,000,000 school construction program is also under way.

Women's Bar Group Will Meet Tonight

The Women's Bar Association will meet at 7.15 o'clock tonight at Hooper's Restaurant, 22 East Fayette street. A dinner at 6 P.M. will precede the meeting.

Mrs. Leona Morris, dean of student personnel of the Baltimore Junior College, will speak on "United Nations in the Sixties."

Left: Announcing the plan for the new town of Columbia, 1963. *From the* Baltimore Sun.

Below: Map of Columbia, 1965. *Central Maryland News.*

Opposite: Article about the encroaching development in 1972. From the *Columbia Villager.*

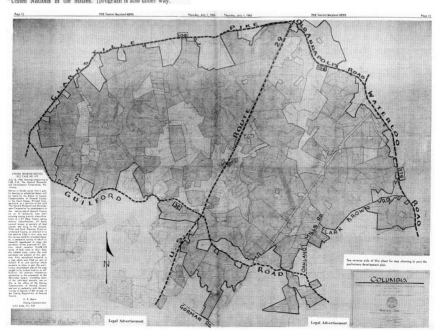

community in just a few years. The plan for an "economically diverse, polycultural, multi-faith and inter-racial" community was as ambitious as the chaos that ensued was predictable.[388] As of 2020, Columbia's population was 104,681, triple the entire population of Howard County in 1960.[389]

One of the issues Rouse faced was needing an employment anchor for Columbia, a company large enough to encourage others to invest and to serve as a base for many of the workers coming to Columbia. After long discussions and the lure of a railroad spur, General Electric–Westinghouse became that anchor in what is, sixty years later, the next focus of mixed-use redevelopment—the Columbia Gateway area.

GUILFORD: THE LITTLE TOWN THAT WOULDN'T DIE

An NPR article from 2021 entitled "A Brief History of How Racism Shaped Interstate Highways" reminded us of what happened to Guilford in the 1960s. Guilford was a nice, quiet community before James Rouse brought his vision for Columbia and its massive development to come. The highway system proposed in the 1960s included both Interstate 95 and State Route 32, and as you can see in the image opposite, those two highways would permanently geographically divide the Guilford community.[390]

In the early 1960s, Rouse Company operatives were gobbling up land under the guise of several different entities, and by 1965, Charles E. Miller was leading the approval to rezone all of Columbia so development could begin. These plans included making Route 32 into a full expressway. Shortly after Guilford Elementary School was desegregated, the plans for a new interstate through the northeast corridor were becoming a reality.[391]

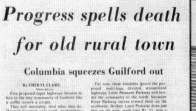

Progress spells death for old rural town

Columbia squeezes Guilford out

By CHERYL CLARK
News editor

Five proposed super highways threaten to box in the tiny community of Guilford like a coffin covers a corpse.

They will inevitably. And when they do, Howard County's only rural, predominantly black quarry town will be gone forever.

It seems to the 500 residents who've outlasted the surrounding "progress", that God has completely forgotten them. At best, they say, he's certainly giving them a test.

Almost daily, someone in the community is approached by a real estate broker who offers a "bargain deal" for sale of their property. Many families, probably numbering 100 people, have taken them up on their offer and church membership has dropped accordingly.

For now, these residents ignore the proposed multi-lane, divided, streamlined highways. Little Patuxent Parkway will border the community to the north. Snowden River Parkway curves toward them on the northwest, Broken Land Parkway does just that on the west, multi-lane Rt. 32, now a wobbly 32 foot wide road, will literally cut through the community on the south. Interstate 95 now provides an eastern border.

And three more super-duper highways draw another concentric horseshoe around Guilford. They are Rt. 1, scheduled for widening in the future, the proposed Outer Beltway and Old Columbia Pike or Rt. 29. All will be less than four miles from the tiny town.

What was once an active town for granite quarry workers still provides an amazing contrast with all that hustle bustle.

A doll seems to stare forlornly out the window in this dying rural town, Guilford.

In 1967, it was reported that I-95 and its interchange with Route 32 would displace about eleven of the forty Black families in Guilford. The *Baltimore Sun* article reporting on this quoted the State Roads Commission: "They would not be able to find housing in Howard County that would be acceptable and that they could afford."[392] The State Roads Commission offered to provide fair market value for the homes of those being displaced (which ended up being eight families), but the relocation site chosen along Mission Road was described as "swampy." The State Roads Commission agreed to provide proper drainage for the land, and four of the residents agreed to be relocated. The disposition of the other four families is not certain.

Between the encroachment of the new Columbia development and the building of I-95 and the exchange with Route 32, the situation was dire for Guilford in 1972. In February, the *Columbia Villager*, a paper that lasted only two years, published the headline "Progress Spells Death for Our Rural Town—Columbia Squeezed Guilford Out."[393] It was reported that 20 percent of the residents sold their land to developers as development of the General Electric Plant and the Guilford Industrial Center closed in on them. Church membership dropped. Talk of a huge Marriott theme park along Vollmerhausen Road didn't help the concerns.

The *Villager* continued, "Although there is little distinction between white and black neighborhoods, residents maintain two racially separate existences which revolve around two churches, one completely black, one completely white. A minister called the town 'pre Martin Luther King.'" Even the future of Guilford Elementary School was in doubt: "Although Guilford school is scheduled for refurbishing in two years, residents don't think there will be a Guilford school next year" due to the drop in population and the "high rate of turnover" of the principals of the school.[394]

Although the Marriott theme park never materialized, the Guilford community was forever changed by I-95 and the interchange with Route 32.[395] Many people from the original families of the community still live there, and the population has grown greatly since the 1970s. In a March 24, 1991 *Washington Post* article called "Patchwork Development Passes by Working Poor," Beaula Moore, who still lives on Guilford Road, was asked how she felt about the encroachment of Columbia's development. She said, "We're fighting to stay as long as we can....We want them [the newcomers] to conform to our ways, not us to conform to them." Fortunately, Moore won and is still there as of this writing; she celebrated her ninety-ninth birthday in June 2023.[396]

Industry encroaching

Howard government pitches in to preserve Guilford character

By MICHAEL J. CLARK
Columbia Bureau of The Sun

The Howard county government has joined with several local groups to try to save the predominantly black community of Guilford just south of Columbia from encroaching industrial development.

"A low-to-moderate income area," Guilford is bounded by industrial uses, the county's Office of Planning and Zoning notes in its recently prepared housing report.

"This 1,600-acre community is under intense pressure for conversion to further industrial land uses. Resistance to these pressures from neighborhood residents and organizations is strong," the report further says.

ble to industry is Interstate 95 right in Guilford's midst, and a railroad spur hooking up with the industry along the community's northern section.

The county planners point out that a 31-acre site in residentially zoned Guilford already is the subject of an application for rezoning for industrial use, and a 22-acre tract near the Guilford Elementary School is for sale.

A county planning staff report says that in the section of Guilford east of the interstate highway only about a third of the 600 acres are owned by local people.

The report says 286 acres there are occupied by the Federal Communications Commission, which operates a moni-

work. A survey of Guilford residents also will be initiated to determine their priorities for the possible redevelopment of the community.

According to Natalie Lobe, a senior county planner, "possibilities for saving Guilford could include introducing more housing, rehabilitating existing substandard housing, as well as developing more community facilities, park land and commercial enterprises."

Mrs. Lobe also observed that "There is low density in Guilford and under the existing residential zoning, as many as 5,000 people could live in the area rather than the 800 to 1,000 people presently there. However, we want to wait until the community survey is made

Howard government pitches in for Guilford, 1973. From the *Baltimore Sun*.

Despite the hardships, this Guilford community is a resilient and proud one. Development continues, but a new high school will open in the fall of 2023 along Mission Road, named Guilford Park High School in honor of the historic Guilford community.

RECOMMISSIONING THE PATUXENT BRANCH RAILROAD

The former Patuxent Branch rail line that has been turned into the popular pedestrian Wincopin Green and Patuxent Branch Trails was almost turned into a railway again in the late 1960s.[397] The railroad was to serve the General Electric (GE) appliance plant that was to be built adjacent to Guilford between the new I-95 and Snowden Boulevard covering what used to be Lark Brown Road. It is now called the Gateway Commerce Center.

One of the most critical parts of Columbia's development was establishing a large business enterprise that would serve as an employment anchor for the new town. An expanse of land owned by Arundel Corporation in eastern Columbia seemed ideal for this venture. Rouse Company sought many potential employers, but only General Electric agreed to anchor Columbia and build a large plant to manufacture and ship appliances. But GE needed a stable means of transportation for its goods and services, and in the 1960s, that still meant the railroad.

According to records at the Columbia Archives, the planning had started by 1966, and in 1967, negotiations were underway with the B&O Railroad to select a route from the Washington Branch Line to the new GE Appliance Park. In October 1967, it was clear that James Rouse preferred the Patuxent Branch Line from Savage through Guilford up Oakland Mills Road to GE. The cost would have been between $1.5 and $2 million.[398]

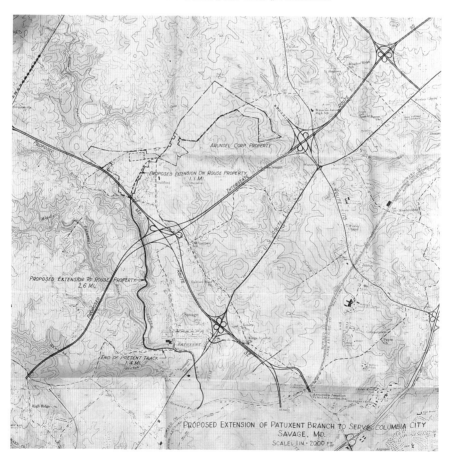

Proposed extension of the Patuxent Branch Rail line, circa 1966. *Columbia Archives.*

An alternative that was proposed went through Annapolis Junction and Waterloo instead, which was the one finally accepted by the B&O. This was called the Columbia Branch railroad. In the summer of 1968, the announcement was made that the new railroad would go from Annapolis Junction over Dorsey Run Road, Route 1 and Mission Road and under I-95.[399] Despite various objections from the community, resulting in legal battles, the GE plant opened in 1971 and closed in 1989.[400] It never created all the jobs planned, and it left the community with a toxic waste legacy as a "Superfund" hazardous waste site.[401]

Today, the former GE site is the Columbia Gateway Innovation District, with over three hundred businesses employing nearly ten thousand.[402] It is planned as a major redevelopment gateway increasing businesses and employment and including residential areas.[403] We wonder if the infrastructure for the Columbia Branch train line will be resurrected for use in the redevelopment plans—the abandoned train tracks and bridges are, surprisingly, still there.

ALTERNATE REALITIES: QUARRIES AND A THEME PARK

The 1960s and 1970s were chaotic times, with the growth of Columbia and the changing of decades-old zoning laws. The Guilford area was on the edge of the new town of Columbia, and uncertainty regarding development was ongoing. What if certain proposals had come to pass? After fifty years, it is easy to see how things actually occurred, but what if they had gone in a different direction?

One of the many granite companies working the Guilford quarries was the West Virginia–incorporated Guilford Granite & Stone Company, which was chartered in 1907 for a fifty-year term.[404] It rose again in 1959 as a Maryland corporation.[405] The company purchased some land it had previously worked along the Little Patuxent River and, in 1965, sought to change the zoning to once again operate a granite quarry.[406] Guilford Granite and Stone petitioned to rezone 315 acres at the intersection of Murray Hill and Guilford Roads (then Route 32) to a heavy industrial use, with 250 trucks a day visiting the site. The actual quarry would have been about 60 acres.[407] Fortunately for the area that would become the Huntington neighborhood as well as the site of Hammond High School, their zoning application was denied in February 1966.[408]

It didn't take long before a similar proposal was made. Contee Sand and Gravel was a long-established company in the area that operated out of Laurel and gambled that a 1967 merger with Guilford Granite and Stone, Percon and Howard-Montgomery Crushed Stone would get that elusive zoning change and a permit for a quarrying operation.[409] The influence of the Gudelsky family, who owned Contee Sand and Gravel and were also one of the major landowners to sell to Howard Research and Development to get Columbia started a few years earlier, set the stage for another proposal that "rocked" Guilford.

In 1969, Contee Sand and Gravel Company proposed a large new 377-acre granite operation on the boundaries of the new Columbia just south of Route 32 in Guilford. It was said to be a proposal for the immediate area along Murray Hill and Vollmerhausen Roads.[410] The quarry itself would be sixty-one acres, like the last proposal. But the Rouse Company as well as its subsidiary, Howard Research and Development, had lawyers at the HoCo Zoning Board of Appeals hearing to oppose the plan. The zoning was for residential use in an area planned to be another Columbia neighborhood. Concerns included dust, heavy-duty traffic and noise, all leading to lower land values in the area.[411]

It also didn't help knowing the effects on the communities near the Savage quarry operated by Arundel Corporation, which was having its own zoning board appeals hearing on its permit that would lead to the closing of that quarry. The Maryland court of appeals had found the Savage quarry to be operating illegally since 1953—it is now called Stone Lake, with a gated community surrounding it.[412] After eleven hearings were held on the matter, the request by Contee Sand and Gravel was denied by the appeals board in April 1970.[413] The effect on the area would have been disastrous, including entire communities here today that would not have existed, including the area high school. Huntington Park would never have been built.

With the matter of turning Guilford into a quarry behind us, the community then learned of a proposal to turn it into an amusement park! In January 1972, Marriott announced its intention to build a massive, $65 million "Marriott's Great America" theme park, to open about 1975.[414] The 850-acre park would have included a six-hundred-room hotel, a shopping plaza and areas for education, recreation and amusement, with eleven million visitors a year and 3,500 jobs once it opened. So where would it be? Guilford, of course.

The plan would have covered the area between I-95 on the east, the new Route 32 on the north, an extended Broken Land Parkway on the west (it

Columbia Villager

Thursday, Jan. 27, 1972   Columbia, Md.   Vol. I, No. 25

'Disneyland' complex to locate here

WASHINGTON – The Marriott Corp., a giant in the hotel-restaurant field, will build a $65 million Disneyland-style entertainment complex on 650 acres owned by the Rouse Co. just a few miles from Columbia.

Gov. Marvin Mandel made the announcement at a press conference here yesterday morning. He noted there will be nearly 50 million people in the New York to Norfolk market area by 1975, the park's first full year of operation.

The Rouse property, located at the Rt. 32 interchange with I-95, was once considered as a site for a sports stadium, possibly for the restless Baltimore Colts. The first phase of entertainment complex

to be called "Marriott's Great America," will have four basic divisions, each totalling about 100 acres. An adventure park with rides and amusements is planned as the largest component, along with a marine life park, a drive-through animal preserve and a New Orleans-type plaza with shops and restaurants.

J. W. Marriott Jr., the firm's president, said a 600-room hotel will also be built. The park will help make Maryland one of the great tourist states, he added.

Marriott predicted that five million people would visit the complex in its first full year and said the number will double in later years as more phases of the park are completed.

Work will begin on the 450-acre phase one development this fall, with opening set for 1974. "We want to be ready for the expected rush of tourists to the east coast and to the Washington area by the 1976 Bicentennial Year," Marriott said.

"Marriott's Great America" will employ about 3,500 people and draw heavily on area youth for personnel, he said. He expects the park to generate $90 million in tax revenue during the period from 1975 to 1984 and he estimates the total economic impact during the same period will be $1.3 billion.

Marriott plans to spend $1 million landscaping the development. Portions of the park will operate from early April to late

November. The enclosed shopping plaza and campgrounds will be open all year and the African animal preserve will be open from March through December.

The adventure park will recreate history in six regional attractions, including Rural America, Old New England, a Midwestern County Fair, the Ante-Bellum South, the Old Southwest and the Klondike.

Rides will include antique autos, a carousel and steam calliope, a steam engine railway. One admission price to the park will entitle visitors to unlimited rides and entertainment for the day.

The marine life park will feature a giant aquarium and a large lake with views from

glassed-in vantage points below its level. Performances by dolphins, whales and sharks are planned.

The animal preserve will present beasts in their natural habitat, Marriott said, while visitors ride through in glass-roofed trams. Trained animal shows and a children's farm animal area will be included.

The Marriott Corp., began with a rootbeer stand in Washington D.C. in the early 1930's and has risen to sales of $347 million in 1971. The corporation, founded by the current president's father, J. Willard Marriott in 1927, now encompasses Hot Shoppes restaurants, hotels and motels in several major cities and a fleet of cruise ships.

The *Columbia Villager* reports on the proposed Marriott theme park, 1972.

Marriott's Park Debated

CHAMP Vs. CRAMP: Chump Insurance Plan?

By David Lightman

To counter CRAMP, there is now Champ dedicated to seeing Howard county residents aren't taken for chumps.

Champ is Countians Happy About Marriott's Park. CRAMP is County Residents Against the Marriott Proposal. CRAMP is about a month old. CHAMP formed Monday.

Irving Metzler and William T. Healy, of Ellicott City, said that CHAMP will "tell the story about Marriott's Great America to all citizens of the county."

Amusement Park

The Marriott Park will be an 850-acre amusement com-

logical study will be made in the sea life park. Also, business education will be constantly obvious, and the American heritage theme of the park will be educational.

4. Preservation of the site. "Very little will be done to change the natural surroundings—thus maintaining the open spaces features now enjoyed by not having the land developed," CHAMP says.

Recreation Facilities

5. Entertainment and recreation. CHAMP members say they are negotiating with Marriott to consider facilities

to benefit county residents only.

6. County services. Business generated by the park will help county businessmen.

Mr. Healy noted, "we're not looking for any dues or expecting to hold many meetings. We only want citizens to come forth and be identified so that our silent majority will have a voice in the community."

Mr. Metzler is a plant foremean at PPG industries, Frederick road, Baltimore. Mr. Healy is an electrical engineer at Goddard Space Center, Greenbelt, Md.

CHAMP or CRAMP? This article about the proposed Marriott theme park was published in 1972. *From the* Evening Sun.

was never completed that far) and the Middle Patuxent River on the south. The community was split over whether the Marriott Park would be a good thing or not. It included two groups with interesting acronyms: CRAMPS (Columbia Residents Against Marriott Proposal) and CHAMPS (Citizens Happy About Marriott Park). One thing is for certain: our future home would have been a parking lot, and we certainly would not have moved here! At least it was better than a quarry.[415]

Hearings began in June 1972, and by September, the plans had been rejected by the HoCo zoning board. The entire area, even region, wouldn't have been the same if a theme park like this had been built. But we also wonder if the economic benefits might have made it worthwhile. Looking at the neighborhoods surrounding other theme parks, we probably would have been taken for a long and winding ride.[416]

What if the granite quarries in Guilford once again became active in either of the proposals put forth? We could have had the equivalent of the enormous Savage Stone quarry off Mission Road. The school board would have sought a different location for Hammond High School, and Kings Contrivance may not have developed as one of the Columbia villages. The original plan for an amusement park would never have allowed the development of the Huntington neighborhood that was attractive enough to move into. Perhaps we never would have moved to Columbia if the Guilford area was industrially developed or became an entertainment district. Who knows what would have become of the area with these alternate realities?

ALTERNATE REALITIES: A LANDFILL AND A THEME PARK (AGAIN)

Looking at more developments that would have forever changed the character of the Guilford, Columbia and HoCo areas, a landfill was proposed, as well as a second round for a Marriott theme park. They just didn't give up without a fight.

One of the six sites considered for a new county landfill was in Guilford between Mission Road and Route 1, just south of where Marriott wanted to build. If Vollmerhausen Road had been extended, that would have run right into the proposed site for a landfill. It was called the Chase Manhattan property and covered about five hundred acres. It was also a predominantly Black community, and as the Reverend John Wright of the First Baptist

Church of Guilford told the county council, "If you were living in Guilford, would you want a landfill beside your home?"[417]

Fortunately for Guilford residents, the papers said that "the public works chief all but said the odds should be against the use of that [Guilford's] site because of a high acquisition cost, a possible negative impact on the water quality of streams in the area and a relatively high haulage cost because of its distance from the county's population center." But perhaps the real reason it wasn't suitable was that it would bring in more revenue from property taxes, about $1.3 million a year, than it would as a landfill.[418]

The Guilford community was strongly against a landfill, as was the upscale Burleigh Manor community. The county eventually selected a different, undeveloped, five-hundred-acre site near where Interstate 70 and Route 40 meet by Marriottsville Road west of Columbia.[419] If the Chase Manhattan site had been chosen as a landfill, Marriott would not have come back to Columbia to make a second pitch for its park. And a new high school and elementary school wouldn't have been built on the site.

With the Chase Manhattan property free again, Marriott swooped in with another proposal a month later. It wanted the 530-acre site for a scaled-down version of what it had proposed five years earlier, with an annual attendance of just 2.6 instead of the previously projected 11 million.[420] The Guilford Steering Committee, representing a portion of the community, supported the proposal and the addition of those jobs—3,000 summer jobs and 250 part-time and 300 full-time year-round jobs—but wanted more information before making any recommendations.[421] The Rouse Company, the HoCo Chamber of Commerce and the mayors of two other Marriott towns came in to support the proposal, but local concern was expressed about whether those 3,000 summer jobs would be available to county youth or mostly go to kids outside of the area.[422]

While there were no groups called CHAMPS or CRAMPS campaigning for or against the Marriott proposal this time, the community seemed decidedly against it, and the HoCo Zoning Board rejected the proposal in a 3–1 vote, saying the proposal lacked "proper safeguards" for the community.[423] Additional concerns were lack of infrastructure, such as for water and sewage, and adequate traffic controls on the trucks using Route 1, which bordered the property. Marriott never got to build its third theme park and, in 1984, sold its Chicago-area amusement park business to Bally Manufacturing Company, owner of Six Flags, and its California park to the City of Santa Clara.[424]

Two Huntington neighborhoods, one on either side of I-95, were built, one of which became our home. Vollmerhausen Road still crosscuts the community between Murray Hill and Guilford Roads. In the late 1980s, an elementary school and middle school were built along Vollmerhausen and Savage-Guilford Road, and I-95 didn't require an exit to and from Vollmerhausen Road, maintaining peaceful local traffic.

When Wincopin Park was opened, the Green Trail was created from the old Patuxent Branch Railroad. The Patuxent Branch Trail now connects Savage Mill with Lake Elkhorn, thanks to the renovation of the Guilford Quarry Pratt Through Truss Bridge for pedestrians. These trails are among the most popular in the region.

Immediately east of the Chase Manhattan property, a quarry was finally built after years of trying to obtain a permit. In 2004, the state approved a mining permit for the 545-acre site. As a concession to the community near the quarry, the beautiful Ridgely Run Community Center was established.

The Chase Manhattan property was sold to HoCo to build a badly needed high school in the southeastern part of HoCo that will likely result in a boost in property values. The first new HoCo high school in twenty years opened in the fall of 2023, and it is named Guilford Park High School. Had the Chase property become the county landfill or the site for an amusement park, there certainly would never have been an opportunity to build this high school. We still wonder, though: what if?

Chapter 11

A Forgotten Cemetery

HoCo has recorded 204 cemeteries within its boundaries, including family, corporate and abandoned cemeteries and some that no longer exist. The Coalition to Protect Maryland Burial Sites has been active in HoCo, in particular with an abandoned and forgotten cemetery we rediscovered. We called it the Guilford Quarry Cemetery due to its proximity to the quarries, but we soon discovered family origins for this quarter-acre plot of land as well as some of the burials within it. Volunteers, cemetery experts, preservationists and even the Maryland State Highway Administration assisted in clearing weeds and other debris from the cemetery. Chesapeake Search Dogs, a volunteer search and rescue team with cadaver dogs, held a training session at the cemetery. The cadaver dogs consistently picked up the scent of human remains near trees and depressions in the ground throughout the site. They even caught a scent beyond the fence line of Route 32, whose property belongs to the State Highway Administration. Mapping of stones and GPR (ground-penetrating radar) were also used at the site. But these discoveries have not been enough to sustain the interest or action of specialists who could take this research further. Perhaps someone reading these stories will be inspired to action.

ELIZAMA RLOWWAS

The first headstone we were able to see when exploring the overgrown piece of land containing the graveyard in 2018 belonged to Eliza Marlow.

Left: Eliza Marlow headstone, 1838. *Right*: John Carroll headstone, 1829. *Author's collection.*

The headstone was not easy to read, and we couldn't make sense of the name. The stone was caked in dirt, and we used the hard stem of one of the thorny plants growing over the grounds to clean it. The first line was E-L-I-Z-A-M-A, and the second was R-L-O-W-W-A-S. As this was the first old headstone we had ever tried to read, we thought what a strange name it was and wondered who Elizama Rlowwas could be. We soon realized it read "Eliza Marlow was born June 28, 1802 / Died Sept 18, 1838." This was our first clue for the cemetery, and we were excited! Now for the research.

It didn't take long before a Google search led us to a record in MacKenzie's 1917 *Colonial Families of the United States of America* that matched Eliza's birth and death dates as they appeared on the headstone.[425] Eliza Marlow was born Eliza Isaac, of Ellicott City, and in December 1821, she married John Carroll from the Guilford area.[426] John and Eliza Carroll had two children—William Henry and Charles—before John Carroll died on December 9, 1829.[427] Oddly, his last will and testament was dated December 10.

John's will was clear that he wanted his two sons to be deeded the land they were living on. He was also clear that Eliza should live there and raise their sons or have his good friend William Moore become their sons' legal guardian. John wrote: "I give and bequeath all of the Estate of whatsoever kind or nature it may be whether Real, personal or mixed, to be equally divided between my said two sons William Henry and Charles, share and share alike." Regarding his land, he wrote, "Whereas I purchased the lot or parcel of land whereon I now reside containing three and three fourths acres of land more or less of John G. Proud…it is my Will and desire that he should Execute a Deed in fee simple for the same to my two sons William Henry Carroll and Charles Carroll, reserving to my wife Eliza Carroll her life Estate in the same."[428]

A March 1, 1830 deed from John G. Proud to William Henry and Charles Carroll fulfilled the wish in John Carroll's will. It also showed that at the time of John's death, the Carrolls lived on the northeast corner of Wincopin within an easy walk of the graveyard. The deed also revealed that Carroll was doing blacksmith work for Proud as payment for the land.[429]

In 1830, Eliza was living with her two sons, both under the age of five, and a woman between fifteen and twenty who was possibly her sister.[430] She also had two enslaved girls listed in the household. Eliza lived on the land with her two boys until she remarried to Benjamin Marlow on February 18, 1832.[431] They had two children of their own before she died—George W. Marlow (b. 1833) and Sarah Ellen Marlow (b. 1835).[432]

What happened to Eliza and their children? Eliza Carroll stayed on the land when she married Benjamin Marlow and raised her two sons along with the two children she had with Benjamin Marlow. The headstone of M.A. Marlow (May 1837–July 1838), their third child, who died just two months before Eliza, indicates they lived there when the child died. Another stone with just the initials MAM visible may also be another Marlow stone.

What happened after Eliza died? John's good friend William Moore kept his promise to find a guardian for the children. On October 18, one month after Eliza's death, he submitted a request to the courts to have "their friend and uncle David Carroll of Baltimore County" be their guardian. This was approved in December 1838.[433]

Not only were John and David Carroll brothers, but they also grew up together in Guilford. This is why David's infant son, Thomas Lemuel Carroll, is also buried in the cemetery next to Eliza. The 1840 census shows that David Carroll had two boys between the ages of ten and fifteen as well as his own infant son living with him in Baltimore. It looks like William Henry and Charles were well taken care of.[434]

On the day of Eliza's death, David Carroll made an agreement with Benjamin Marlow that Marlow could stay on the land for one year as long as he paid rent and did some repairs on the property.[435] It is likely Marlow

William Moore requesting David Carroll become guardian of William Henry and Charles Carroll, 1838. *HoCo Orphans Court.*

stayed on the land with the two children he had with Eliza until he moved to his own property. In 1840, Benjamin Marlow married Eliza's younger sister Mary Ann, and they were living with two young children, presumably George and Sarah, next to his father's property.[436]

George ended up living in Guilford and working as a farmer, according to the 1860 census. George and his wife, Julia, were also raising Mary Lowry, the daughter of quarryman Amon Lowry, who died in 1855.[437] Amon Lowry was a partner of Henry Penny and ran the Guilford quarry in 1850, so there must have been an established relationship among the Marlow, Lowry and Penny families. Henry Penny sold some Guilford land to George Marlow, and in 1870, George was listed in the census as a stone cutter.[438]

Eliza's brothers, Thomas Jefferson, George Washington, Zedekiah Moore and William Andrew Jackson, lived in Ellicott City most of their lives. William Andrew Jackson Isaac went mostly by A.J. or A. Jackson and became a granite quarrier in Ellicott City. Zedekiah was a stone mason, and George was a blacksmith. Their oldest brother, Thomas, was a carpenter like their father and lived in Ellicott City.[439]

Thomas also owned and rented out the land that the "Log Cabin" (sometimes called the Thomas Isaac Log Cabin) had been built on. Ironically, Thomas Isaac never lived in the cabin or on the land it was located on, but politicians back in the 1970s decided it should be named after Thomas Isaac instead of the Black families that originally lived in the cabin or that were the last ones to reside in it. Levi Gillis, a Black minister, is believed to have built the Log Cabin on its original Merryman Street site.

Zedekiah also served as mayor of Ellicott during the time in which it was incorporated as a city, and his brother George served the Howard County courts as their crier for over thirty years, a position their father, John, had previously held.[440] This certainly was an Ellicott City family.

DAVID CARROLL: FROM SAVAGE TO WOODBERRY

While pulling weeds and cleaning the site in April 2020, we discovered a gravestone at the Guilford Quarry Cemetery that read, "In Memory of Thomas Lemuel Carroll, son of David and Ann Carroll who departed this life July 29th 1836, age 6 months & 22 days."[441] We didn't expect to find an infant's gravestone. Who were David and Ann Carroll? We found a likely pairing in Baltimore County, and the rest of the story followed.

David Carroll was born on May 30, 1811, in Guilford along the Little Patuxent River, not far from the SMC.[442] In 1828 and 1829, there were numerous advertisements for employment under Daniel Hack, a machinist at the "Savage Cotton Factory."[443] On April 1, 1829, at almost eighteen years of age, David Carroll became an apprentice at the newly formed company. David wrote about this apprenticeship in a notebook he acquired from his brother Zachariah.

David may have been able to "commute" from his home in Guilford, but he wrote that starting on January 8, 1830, he was going to board with a Mrs. Carr for eight dollars per month. But it seems that arrangement was short-lived; he wrote that on March 8, he was going to "set in with" Amos A. Williams, the resident agent of Savage Manufacturing Company.[444]

In May 1831, Daniel Hack left Savage Manufacturing Company, so David Carroll's apprenticeship with him would have ended, but not their cooperation. Hack advertised for machinists at Occoquan, Virginia, where he was apparently setting up a new cotton mill.[445]

Carroll wrote in his notebook that in June 1832, he worked with Daniel Hack at Occoquan, where he undoubtedly put into full practice all he learned in his apprenticeship. He wrote about walking between Alexandria and Occoquan, which would have been a distance of about seventeen miles and taken around six hours. Maybe our ancestors did walk five miles to school, uphill both ways! He also wrote that from August 4 to 9, 1832, he lost time at Occoquan due to being at Savage, presumably to work. He was working building cotton looms and other equipment in Savage during at least September 1834 through April 1836, according to his record book.

Thomas Lemuel Carroll headstone, 1836. *Author's collection.*

David married Ann Elizabeth Ayler in Baltimore on October 12, 1833.[446] David and Ann started a family in January 1836, but sadly, their first child, Thomas Lemuel Carroll, died in July at almost seven months old. Thomas Lemuel is buried in the Guilford quarry cemetery.[447] Their first daughter was born in December 1838 in Baltimore. David left Guilford with his wife to make his fortunes in cotton mill businesses such as Woodberry Factory, White Hall Factory and finally Mount Vernon Mills in the Baltimore area. David Carroll's personal and real estate property was valued at $800,000 at the time of his death.[448]

African American Burials in Guilford Cemetery

HoCo historian Beulah (Meacham) Buckner (1930–2005) identified a probable cemetery with enslaved people next to the Guilford Quarry in 1982, and it became listed in the HoCo Cemetery Inventory as F-82-096. On October 20, 1989, Buckner prepared a list of twenty-seven "African American Graves in Howard County" and noted that cemetery no. 17 (Guilford cemetery didn't have a name then) was an "old cemetery believed to be a slave burial—Jedadiah 1826" behind 9135 Guilford Road.[449]

Buckner was able to discern just a couple of graves on this heavily overgrown site, less than an acre in size, but visits by various officials in 2018 revealed up to eighty or so burials in this cemetery, and another visit in 2020 indicated that the number of burials is likely higher. The many granite fieldstones marking the heads and foots of the grave sites, lack of engraved headstones, graves aligned and facing east, dogwood and growths of periwinkle, pre–Civil War burials and proximity to the main Guilford quarry all strongly suggest that many of the burials in this cemetery were of enslaved people.[450]

It seems that this cemetery contains burials of both White and Black people, although we have yet to determine how many African Americans are buried there or who they could be. We have scoured records at the Maryland State Archives and our local private historical society, asked elderly residents and researchers and looked through county land records but have no remaining clues to follow. Perhaps we haven't looked hard enough specifically for "Jedadiah 1826," or perhaps we missed some clues. We have also done a complete chain of title for the cemetery ownership, hoping records of past owners would shed light on the occupants of the graveyard, but we have found no clues. As more records are made available online and more people become aware of this cemetery, perhaps we will learn more. But for now, our cemetery is like dozens, hundreds or thousands of others across the county—hidden and forgotten.

LONELY CIVIL WAR GRAVE SITE

We thank local friends and fellow history explorers Barb and Liam, as they brought us to a unique and isolated burial site belonging to a Civil War veteran named John Francis Wyman, more commonly called Frank. This site is located overlooking the Middle Patuxent River downstream of Murray Hill Road and just upstream of Interstate 95.

Wyman served in Company F, First Regiment, New York Lincoln Cavalry, starting as a private and mustering out as a quartermaster sergeant. In the cavalry, he was also part of the Mounted Rifles unit. Their company's notable battles were the skirmish at Upperville, Virginia, on February 20, 1864, and the Battle of New Market, Virginia, on May 15, 1864.[451]

According to the information at the site, Wyman was born in Syracuse, New York, and married Hester Anne Morehead of Fauquier, Virginia, on December 31, 1866. They had one child to our knowledge, William Howard Wyman. Wyman died in a train accident at Annapolis Junction station (currently called the Savage station) on July 7, 1880. Wyman was working

John Francis Wyman grave site, 1880. *Author's collection.*

for the U.S. Census Bureau and living in Washington, D.C., having recently been separated from his wife, who was still living in HoCo.

The July 8, 1880 *Evening Star* newspaper reported on Wyman's gruesome train accident at Annapolis Junction. He was struck by the cowcatcher on the front of a train that was passing the station while another train was stopped. He was pushed into the air and landed headfirst on the platform. He was taken to a hospital in Washington, D.C., where he died early the next morning. A year later, a lawsuit was filed by the HoCo government against the B&O Railroad on behalf of Hester Wyman, his widow, and in 1882, a judgement of $1,500 was granted to Hester Wyman and her son, William.[452]

Hester Wyman remarried in 1885 to Austin C. Sweet, but apparently theirs was an unhappy marriage, and she filed for divorce in September 1892. But just a few months later, on November 29, Sweet died, and the case was dismissed. The now Mrs. Sweet petitioned to change her name back to Wyman because "no children were born to her as the wife of Sweet, while as Mrs. Wyman she bore several, all of whom are now grown. It is mortifying in the extreme to be obliged to use the second husband's name, says Mrs. Sweet, when the public generally knows her as the mother of the Wyman children." She also claimed her life with Wyman was notably happy and contented. One of the newspaper headlines about her case read "No Longer Wishes to Be Sweet." On September 4, 1900, she was granted her older married name, Hester A. Wyman.[453]

Now that she was Hester A. Wyman again, she continued to focus her energies on the Daughters of the American Revolution group she was involved with. But somewhere along the way, she learned that her second marriage was illegitimate, as Sweet was never divorced from his first wife. Hester filed a lawsuit to "compel the issuance to her of a pension as the widow of J. Frank Wyman, a veteran of the civil war." At the age of seventy-seven, she died as a hit-and-run victim; the driver was never caught.[454]

According to the information at the grave site, Wyman "settled and operated a farm here overlooking the Middle Patuxent River." It appears his wife was still living there when they separated, and it was as good a place as any for his burial. With his grave site located on this beautiful overlook, there is no reason to doubt he was living there before he and his wife separated.

Appendix

Maryland Land Records

MDLANDREC.NET (https://mdlandrec.net/main/index.cfm) is a website maintained by the Maryland State Archives that contains most of the earliest land records up to the present day. These records are mostly deeds but also include leases, agreements and assignments, and some even include plats or maps. Records cover both individuals and corporations and are categorized by county.

To gain access to this valuable resource, a simple account needs to be established online. You can then log into the site whenever you wish to search for records. HoCo records go back to 1840, the year after HoCo was established as a district within Anne Arundel County. Earlier records for our area go back to 1653 under Anne Arundel, but the indexes are at times lengthy and difficult to read.

When we look through these earlier records, which are all done in cursive writing, we certainly lament our school system no longer teaching children to read and write in cursive.

Book Endnotes and Citations

Before we get into the weeds on finding land records in Maryland, we need to acknowledge how important the Maryland State Archives has been to this effort, and so many others. We heavily rely on these land records, and this book therefore has hundreds of citations/endnotes referencing them. To shorten these for the benefit of our readers, we are using a standard shortened format for the citations. One of our longer and more formal citations would be as follows:

Anne Arundel County Court (Land Records). Richard Stringer Deed to Archibald Moncrieff. Guilford Mills. 1792 Sept. 14. NH 6, p. 0550–0551, MSA_CE76_34. Courtesy of the Maryland State Archives. https://plats.msa.maryland.gov/pages/unit.aspx?cid=BA&qualifier=S&series=1213&unit=1527&page=adv1&id=343835565.

A shortened format of this citation will follow the format of Title, Date, Location, Liber (book) and Folio (page). A further description may occur in the endnote if it benefits the reader. So the previous example will be shortened to:

Richard Stringer Deed to Archibald Moncrieff. Guilford Mills, AACo, NH 6, Sept.14, 1792, 550–551.

Getting Started

The following will guide you on your own searches of the online MDLANDREC.

- Go to https://mdlandrec.net/main/index.cfm and establish an account. Once you do that, proceed.
- Select "HoCo" (or whichever county you want) from the dropdown menu.
- Select "active records" on left sidebar.
- You can choose the years you want to look at by grantor (seller) or grantee (buyer). If between 1840 and 1920, they are pretty easy to read and to find.
- You can research them by someone's name, year and sometimes property name.
- If you have one deed, you can find the land record within it and enter the information in the website. Enter the clerk's initials (e.g., www, wsg, nh), book (a.k.a. liber) and page (folio), and you'll be taken to the specific page for the land record. The clerk's initial are optional.

TIPS FOR SEARCHING

- HoCo was part of Anne Arundel County prior to 1851 when HoCo was officially formed. Between 1839 and 1851, it was the Howard District of Anne Arundel County. The land records under HoCo go back to 1840. Prior to 1840, you need to use the Anne Arundel County files.
- If you go further back into the records, HoCo was actually part of Baltimore County between 1698 and 1727. Even if your query is found in the Anne Arundel deeds during that period, you will see many records that identify property as being in Baltimore County.
- Check out the annotated list of HoCo land patents by Jody Frey at https://jsfecmd.info/FREAK/HowardCountyLandPatents. html. The links used to go directly to the land patents but MSA uncoupled those direct links for some reason, believing that they were covered already within the plats.net link in MDLANDREC (few land patent records are there, and they are difficult to find). See our tips for finding land patents outside of mdlandrec below.
- HoCo land patent information (not the patents themselves) can be found through an index listing at http://guide.msa. maryland.gov/pages/series.aspx?ID=S1593. This is a list of the patents in HoCo and provides the clerk, book (liber) and page (folio) that you can look up in MDLANDREC.NET.
- Most of the records have an identifier on the left side of the page in red. As an example, one deed had the following information on this "red ribbon": BALTIMORE COUNTY COURT (Land Records) TK 297, p. 0428, MSA_CE66_347. Date available 05/03/2007. Printed 09/02/2020. This is useful for documenting the information.
- The Anne Arundel County land records has a drop-down option to look at the 1653–1839 records, which covers HoCo before it was officially a county. But it also covers all of Anne Arundel County. A nice feature of this particular set of records is that the land patent name is in the list just as a person's surname is listed. So you could actually search the *W*s for "Wincopin Neck" and the *J*s for "Jones Fancy," etc.

- Please see this video put out by the Maryland State Archives about searching historical land records in MDLANDREC: https://www.youtube.com/watch?v=CmSeIbgwSEU.

Patent Records Not in MDLANDREC.NET

- Index cards were used before digitizing the record. MSA contains an interesting card catalogue scanned into a series of pdf files (see example below). It is not perfect, but it has a lot of information and is a good backup or even a starting place. The cards have the clerk, book and page number for an easy lookup. You can find the patent card index here: https://msa.maryland. gov/msa/stagser/s1400/s1426/html/index54.html.
- Electronically scanned record books are another great source of information. They can be a little intimidating to use but provide some of the oldest patents and land records. Using the information from the index cards described above, you can find the books containing the records. This first link will take you to large pdf files that contain the records listed by clerk and year. This is useful when looking at the patent card index above: http://guide.msa.maryland.gov/pages/series.aspx?id=SE23.
- A list of the patents in HoCo with the clerk, book and page can be looked up in MDLANDREC.NET. You can do some searching (filter criteria) by date, plat and description. This is another useful alterative to peruse, but it does not link directly to any other records: http://guide.msa.maryland.gov/pages/series.aspx?id=S1593.

Mapping Land Patents

Frey's Emporium of Amazing Knowledge, by the amazing Jody Frey, has annotated descriptions of land patents for HoCo, as well as kml files with mapped patent boundaries that can be imported into Google Earth. The time and dedication it took to create these files is truly, well, amazing! Jody did the mapping of both Howard and Anne Arundel County land patents. Check out her "museum"; you won't be disappointed: https://jsfecmd.info/FREAK/Museum.html.

Maryland Inventory of Historic Properties

The Maryland Historical Trust inventory can be searched with Maryland's Cultural Resource Information System (MEDUSA), https://mht. maryland.gov/secure/medusa/, to find documentation on properties recorded in the Maryland Inventory, including architectural information on historic properties and information on archaeological investigations. There are 1,283 HoCo listings under "architecture." You need to have an account to view information on archaeology. Please note that the Maryland Historical Trust is not a history-based organization but one focused on architecture and archaeology. History documented in these forms always needs to be verified.

NOTES

Chapter 1

1. "Columbia Named Best Place in Maryland to Raise a Family and Live," Howard County Press Release, July 5, 2023, https://www.howardcountymd.gov/News070523.
2. "Maryland at a Glance: Native Americans," Maryland State Archives, 2022, https://msa.maryland.gov/msa/mdmanual/01glance/native/html/01native.html.
3. "Land Acknowledgements," Maryland State Arts Council, 2023, https://msac.org/resources/land-acknowledgements.
4. The State of Maryland, Executive Order 01.01.2012.02, "Recognition of the Maryland Indian Status of the Piscataway Indian Nation," 2012.
5. "Land Acknowledgment Resources," University of Maryland, Baltimore County Office of Equity and Inclusion, 2020, https://oei.umbc.edu/land-acknowledgement-statement/.
6. Fern Shen, "A 1652 Treaty Opens Up the Story of the First 'Baltimoreans,'" *Baltimore Brew*, December 10, 2019, https://www.baltimorebrew.com/2019/12/10/a-1652-treaty-opens-up-the-story-of-the-first-baltimoreans/.
7. Hamill Thomas Kenny, *The Origin and Meaning of the Indian Place Names of Maryland* (Baltimore: Waverly Press, 1961), 105–7.
8. "Land Records," Maryland State Archives, http://guide.msa.maryland.gov/pages/viewer.aspx?page=landrecords#mdlandrec.

9. Joseph Foster, "Foster's Fancy Certificate," 100 acres, Anne Arundel County, Liber 12, May 11, 1670, 311; William Ebden, "Hockley Certificate," 100 acres, AACo, Liber 12, August 7, 1670, 308.

10. Major General John Hammond, "Rich Neck," 284 acres, AACo, Liber 22, March 20, 1685, 183; Colonel Henry Ridgely, "Ridgely's Forrest Certificate," 264 acres, AACo, C3, June 3, 1686, 338.

11. Filby, *Savage, Maryland*, 9.

12. Mathews, *Counties of Maryland*, 509–11.

13. Ibid.

14. Ibid., 438.

15. Martenet, *Map of Maryland*.

16. William Hand Browne (ed.), *Archives of Maryland. Proceedings and Acts of the General Assembly of Maryland. March 1697/8–July 1699* (Baltimore: Maryland Historical Society, 1902), 147–48.

17. Mathews, *Counties of Maryland*, 446.

18. Elizabeth Janney, *Elkridge*, Images of America series (Charleston, SC: Arcadia Publishing, 2003).

19. Joetta M. Cramm, *Howard County: A Pictorial History* (Virginia Beach, VA: Donning, 2004), 25

20. Warfield, *Founders*, 337; Robert Schnepfe Diggs, *The Early History of Elkridge Landing* (College Park, MD: University of Maryland, 1937), 1–2. Available at the Internet Archive.

21. Joseph Foster, "Foster's Fancy Certificate"; William Ebden, "Hockley Certificate."

22. Adam Shipley, "Adam the First Certificate," 500 acres, AACo, Liber 22, April 8, 1687, 313.

23. Tyson, *Settlement of Ellicott's Mills*, 5.

24. "Chapter III. An Act for Erecting a Town at and about the Landing, Called the Elk-Ridge Landing, Near the Head of the Patapsco River, in Anne-Arundel County." Passed April 12, 1733. https://msa.maryland.gov/megafile/msa/speccol/sc2900/sc2908/000001/000075/html/am75--419.html.

25. 1753. "Chapter XXVII. An Act to Prevent Injuring the Navigation to Baltimore-Town, and to the Inspecting House at Elk-Ridge Landing, on Patapsco River." Passed 17th of November 1753. Liber HS Folio 117. In 1799. *The Laws of Maryland*. Vol. 1. Annapolis.

26. *Niles Weekly Register*, "Elk Ridge Landing," vol. 28 (May 7, 1825), 159.

27. Henry Ridgely, "Ridgely's Forrest Certificate," 1868; Henry Ridgely III, "Harry's Lott Certificate," 703 acres, AACo, EI5, 1734, 161;

Richard Warfield, "Wincopin Neck Certificate," 864 acres, AACo, EI3, 1735, 482; John Jones, "Jones Fancy Certificate," 131 acres, AACo, EI3, 1734, 76; Joseph Hall, "Hall's Lott Certificate," 128 acres, AACo, BC & GB1, 1753, 208; Richard Warfield, "Warfield's Contrivance Certificate and Patent," 375 acres, AACo, FF7, 374–75; Joseph White, "Whites Fortune Certificate," 268 acres, AACo, EI3, 1734, 79; Joseph White III, "White's Contrivance Certificate," 801 acres, AACo, IC #N, 173, patented to Griffith White, IC #L, 1797, 236.

28. 1728. "Chapter XV. An Act for Erecting a New Parish Out of That Part of St. Paul's Parish That Lies in Anne-Arundel County, and Out of All-Hallow's and St. Anne's Parishes in the Said County." Passed 24th of October 1728. In 1799. *The Laws of Maryland*. Vol. 1. Annapolis.

29. Lucy H. Harrison, *Christ Church, Queen Caroline Parish, Anne Arundel County, Now Howard County, Maryland*, Vestry Meeting Minutes of November 27, 1728, and May 15, 1729 (Salt Lake City, UT: Genealogical Society of Utah, 1949). https://www.familysearch.org/ark:/61903/3:1:3Q9M-CS3L-4QSS-K?mode=g&cat=91565.

30. Ibid.

31. "The Town of Guilford: Patuxent Branch Trail," Guilford historical marker, Historical Marker Database, accessed July 2, 2021, https://www.hmdb.org/marker.asp?marker=19884.

32. Richard Ridgely Indenture to Joseph Conman, "Guilford Tract," 1393 acres, General Court of the Western Shore, Maryland (Land Records), JG1, June 5, 1789, 351–54, courtesy of the Maryland State Archives.

33. Richard Stringer Deed to Archibald Moncrieff. "Guilford Mills," AACo, NH 6, September 14, 1792, 0550–51.

34. John and Mary Polton Deed to Richard Ridgely, AACo, NH 2, September 8, 1785, 0295–97.

35. Courtland T. Reid, *Guilford Courthouse National Military Park, North Carolina*, National Park Service Historical Handbook Series No. 30. (Washington, D.C.: Government Printing Office, 1959; reprinted 1961), 21, 30, http://npshistory.com/handbooks/historical/30-1961.pdf.

36. William Hand Browne (ed.), *Journal and Correspondence of the Maryland Council of Safety, August 29, 1775 to July 6, 1776* (Baltimore: Maryland Historical Society, 1892), 191, http://aomol.msa.maryland.gov/000001/000011/html/am11--192.html; Fold3 records of Thomas Iams and Marmaduke S. Davies, who served under Captain Stringer; U.S. Revolutionary War Records search, Fold3.com; accessed July 2,

2021; https://www.fold3.com/image/14062573 and https://www.fold3.com/image/24192550.

37. Paul J. Gilman D'Arcy, "A Baltimore Estate: Guilford and Its Three Owners," *Maryland Historical Magazine* 51, no. 1, March 1956, 14; "Guilford Community History," Guilford Association: Baltimore's Premier Residential Community, https://guilfordassociation.org/community/history/.

38. G.M. Hopkins, *Atlas of Fifteen Miles Around Baltimore Including Howard Co, Maryland* (Philadelphia: G.M. Hopkins, 1878), http://jhir.library.jhu.edu/handle/1774.2/32620.

39. Record of Appointment of Postmasters, 1832–September 30, 1971. Maryland, Allegany-Frederick Counties, National Archives, Roll 55, Volume 43, 1973, 698.

40. The Gary Manufacturing Company Deed to August Brunner, HoCo, JHO 61, 0358, April 12, 1894.

41. Record of Appointment of Postmasters, 1832–September 30, 1971. Maryland. Allegany-Frederick Counties. National Archives, Roll 55, Volume 62. 1973, 465–66.

42. Record of Appointment of Postmasters. 1789–1832. Record of First Returns Received from Postmasters, October 1789–July 1818. National Archives, Microform Publication M1131, Roll 1, 1973, 172–73.

43. Record of Appointment of Postmasters. 1832–September 30, 1971. Maryland. Allegany-Frederick Counties. National Archives, Roll 55, Volume 9. 1973, 5.

44. Record of Appointment of Postmasters. October 1789–1832. 1824–1828. Roll 3. National Archives, Microform Publication M1131. Lines 1373 (Cooksville), 2267 (Elk Ridge Landing). 5737 Oakland Mills, 1980.

45. Social Security Administration; Washington D.C., USA; Social Security Death Index, Master File. Beulah M. Buckner. Ancestry.com.

46. Letter from Mrs. Beulah Buckner to Rev. C.E. Mitchell of Locust United Methodist Church, dated 7 December 1988. Held by Howard County Recreations and Parks. Recorded February 4, 2021.

47. Writings in a folder called "Meacham Buckner Collection—Manuscript Drafts" held by Howard County Recreations and Parks. Recorded August 19, 2021.

Chapter 2

48. McGrain, *Molinography of Maryland*.
49. Joseph White, "White's Fortune Patent #1692," 268 acres, AACo, EI 2, June 10, 1734, 130.
50. Warfield, *Founders*, 347.
51. Roscoe R. White, White Family Records—Descendants of Peregrine White 1620–1939 (Clarksburg, West Virginia, 1939).
52. Joseph White Jr., "Mill Land Patent #986," 8½ acres. AACo, BY&GS 4, October 12, 1752, 403.
53. Griffith White, "White's Contrivance Patent #1690," 801 acres, AACo, JC L, January 10, 1797, 236. Land was surveyed October 24, 1759.
54. Griffith, *Map*.
55. Gideon White Deed to John Savage, AACo, WSG 9, January 24, 1823, 233.
56. "Country Store, Grist Mill, Etc., for Rent," *Baltimore Sun*, June 11, 1851.
57. Benjamin and Richard Warfield, "Wincopin Neck Patent," 883 acres, AACo, CD, July 9, 1702, 61; Richard Warfield, "Wincopin Neck Patent #1720," 864 acres, AACo, EI4, November 23, 1735, 367.
58. Agreement between Richard Green and Alexander Warfield, Son of John, Partnership for Building Mill and Race, AACo, RB 2, October 6, 1744, 274.
59. *The State Gazette and Merchants and Farmers' Directory for Maryland and District of Columbia* (Baltimore: Sadler, Drysdale & Purnell, 1871), 627–28.
60. *James Owings v. William Baldwin and George Wheeler*, in Richard W. Gill, *Reports of Cases Argued and Determined in the Court of Appeals—Maryland, Volume 8, Containing Cases in 1849* (Annapolis: Bonsall Printers, 1852), 337.
61. "The Burning of a Cotton Mill," *Baltimore Sun*, August 16, 1890.
62. McGrain, *Howard County Mills*,49–50.
63. Benjamin Griffith, "Mill Seat in Partnership Unpatented Certificate #297," 9 acres, AACo, September 10, 1771, 301.
64. AACo, IB 5, July 5, 1777, 415.
65. AACo, NH 1, October 13, 1781, 202.
66. AACo, NH 6, January 20, 1792, 167.
67. General Court of the Western Shore (Land Records), JG4, September 25, 1797, 623.
68. Anne Arundel County, WSG 17, November 19, 1832, 580.

69. Tyson, *Settlement of Ellicott's Mills*, 7.
70. John F. Hart, "The Maryland Mill Act, 1669–1766: Economic Policy and the Confiscatory Redistribution of Private Property," *American Journal of Legal History* 39, no. 1 (January 1995): 1–24.
71. Anne Arundel County, IB 5, December 31, 1774, 139.
72. Ibid., 57.
73. Marion Balderston and Hortense B.C. Gibson, *Balderston Family History* (1973), 25. John was often referred to in later family documents as "John the Immigrant," an affectionate term since he was thought to be the first of the Balderstons to arrive in America.
74. *Wrightstown Monthly Meeting, Book A, Births and Death 1716–1800. List of Members, 1827* (Bucks County, PA: Wrightstown Monthly Meeting, 1948), 23. https://www.ancestry.com/imageviewer/collections/2189/images/31906_275429-00007. This is an account of the births and burials of the children of John Balderston and Hannah his wife. The other accounts are from the Buckingham Monthly Meetings, Society of Friends. Accessed from Ancestry.com. U.S., Quaker Meeting Records, 1681–1935.
75. Tyson, *Settlement of Ellicott's Mills*, 7.
76. Information in this section comes from Edward C. Papenfuse, Alan F. Day, David W. Jordan and Gregory A. Stiverson, *A Biographical Dictionary of the Maryland Legislature 1635–1789* (Baltimore: Johns Hopkins Press, 1979), 628, and M. Lee Preston Jr., *Archaeology in Howard County and Beyond*, 3rd ed (Baltimore: Chesapeake Book Company, 2020), chapters 6 and 3.

Chapter 3

77. Maryland Historical Trust. 1982. Granite Park, along with Moundland, were built by the Stewart family with Guilford granite found along the Middle Patuxent River.
78. Personal inspection of the abutments of the Bollman Bridge in Savage and the Savage Dam showed their materials to be identical to those of the abutments of the Guilford Quarry Pratt Through Truss Bridge.
79. G.W. Wetherill, G.R. Tilton, G.L. Davis, S.R. Hart and C.A. Hopson, "Age Measurements in the Maryland Piedmont," *Journal of Geophysical Research* 71, no. 8 (1966), 2139–55, https://doi.org/10.1029/JZ071i008p02139.

80. Mathews, "Maryland Building Stones," 151.
81. Putney and Riddle were selling granite sills for railroads as far as Philadelphia by 1837, as shown on page 118 of the October 13, 1837 *Appendix to the Journal of Common Council of the City of Philadelphia* (1838), covering the city expenditures.
82. Mathews, "Maryland Building Stones," 151–53.
83. TrainWeb.org paraphrased the letters of High Riddle and revealed corroborating information, and more, about what we suspected about the motivation of Putney and Riddle and the Guilford Quarries. "B&O Old Main Line," TrainWeb.org, http://www.trainweb.org/oldmainline/omlspur1.htm.
84. Deed of trust between Putney and Riddle to Edward Green, Baltimore County, TK 297, 428, August 9, 1839.
85. HoCo Land Records, 5, January 30, 1845, 394.
86. HoCo Land Records, 6, February 6, 1846, 157; HoCo Land Records, 6, March 7, 1846, 243.
87. "Contribution of Baltimore to the Washington National Monument," *Baltimore Sun*, September 15, 1853.
88. Judith M. Jacob, *The Washington Monument: A Technical History and Catalog of the Commemorative Stones* (Washington, D.C.: National Park Service, 2005): 99.
89. *Baltimore Sun* (January 9, 1902; May 23, 1903; November 16, 1906; July 30, 1911), *Wilmington Evening Journal* (September 11, 1902), *News from Frederick, MD* (April 25, 1908), *Washington Evening Star* (April 17, 1920).
90. *Maryland Geological Survey*, volume 2, (Baltimore: Johns Hopkins Press, 1898), 150–58.
91. Penny Lease Agreement with Smith and Johnson, HoCo, LJW 53, March 27, 1888, 190.
92. Watson, *Granites*, 54–56.
93. Guilford and Waltersville sold their land to John Henry Sieling on November 30, 1912, and Sieling in turn sold it to Louis Perna on June 22, 1923 (Liber 118, Folio 93). The Perna family and others conveyed the 2.79 acres containing the quarry to Howard County on December 20, 1976. This chain of title confirms the location of this quarry.
94. Oliver C. Putney was born in Granite, Maryland, on June 25, 1876, and lived there until about 1911. He owned the Oliver C. Putney Granite Corporation, but we haven't determined the extent of his business at the Waltersville quarry or of his exact relationship with True Putney, who was born seventy-six years earlier.

Chapter 4

95. United States, fourth census, 1820. Records of the 1820 census of manufactures, Maryland, AACo, Union Mill; "Today in History—December 20: First American Cotton Mill," Library of Congress, https://www.loc.gov/item/today-in-history/december-20.

96. United States, fourth census, 1820. Records of the 1820 census of manufactures, Maryland, AACo, Eagle Mill.

97. Thomas W. Griffith, *North American Review, Baltimore* 20, no. 46 (Boston: Cummings, Hilliard, January 1825), 128, https://hdl.handle.net/2027/mdp.39015033827968.

98. "The Gary Family," Albert and Shirley Small Special Collections Library, University of Virginia, https://small.library.virginia.edu/collections/featured/the-taylor-family-collection/the-gary-family/.

99. "Joshua Barney," American Battlefield Trust, https://www.battlefields.org/learn/biographies/joshua-barney.

100. Joshua Barney Patent for First Attempt, 4⅝ acres, AACo, June 30, 1810; Joshua Barney Patent for Mill Race, 2¼ Acres, AACo, March 14, 1811.

101. Nathaniel Williams and Caroline Barney were married on October 14, 1809. Caroline and Nathaniel had seven children, and she died at thirty-eight years old in 1825. Nathaniel remarried to Maria Dalrymple on January 14, 1829.

102. Rebecca Hoskins, "The Death and Interment of Joshua Barney," Historical Society Notes and Documents, *Western Pennsylvania Historical Magazine*, January 1982, https://journals.psu.edu/wph/article/viewFile/3761/3579.

103. Savage Manufacturing Company incorporation occurred during the December 1821 session and was passed on February 22, 1822.

104. Pennsylvania Marriage Records, Harrisburg: Pennsylvania Archives Printed Series, Series 2, Series 6, 1876, 256.

105. Thomas C. Middleton, "List of Baptisms Registered at St. Joseph's Church, Philadelphia. (First Series.) from August 29, 1758, to December 31, 1775," *Records of the American Catholic Historical Society of Philadelphia* 1 (1884–86): 246–350, 386–87, http://www.jstor.org/stable/44207428.

106. "Parcel Details," Mapping West Philadelphia Land Owners in October 1777: A Project Hosted by the University of Pennsylvania Archives, https://maps.archives.upenn.edu/WestPhila1777/view-parcel.php?pid=7042.

107. Thomas C. Middleton, "Pew Register of St. Mary's Church, Philadelphia, Pa., from 1787–1791," *Records of the American Catholic Historical Society of Philadelphia* 5, no. 3 (September 1894): 360; Philadelphia County Register of Wills. Witnesses confirmed the death of Darby Savage on October 4, 1780, in his will proceedings within the May 12, 1780 will.

108. Middleton, September 1894, 373.

109. Dunlap and Claypoole's *American Daily Advertiser* (Philadelphia), August 24, 1787. This was an advertisement for sailing to Antigua and to market Antigua rum.

110. "For Sale or Charter the Ship Hope," *Philadelphia Gazette & Universal Daily Advertiser*, October 16, 1799.

111. "Pennsylvania, U.S., Septennial Census, 1779–1863," Philadelphia, Dock Ward, 1800, Ancestry.com.

112. *Poulson's American Daily Advertiser* (Philadelphia), notice of dissolution of the copartnership of the firm Savage & Dugan effective October 9, 1821, published October 11, 1821.

113. John Savage Burial Vault. Ronaldson Cemetery. Historical Society of Pennsylvania; Philadelphia, Pennsylvania; Historic Pennsylvania Church and Town Records. November 19, 1834; John Savage Will. Courtesy of Philadelphia Register of Wills Office. Book 11, p. 316. July 24, 1830. Last codicil November 20, 1833.

114. *John Hollins, Michael McBain and James Williams vs. George Williams*. Contract to ship cotton from Baltimore to France. Baltimore County Court, Equity Papers. C295-12. April 4, 1816.

115. House Committee to Investigate the Bank of the United States and Twenty-Second Congress (1831–33), *Bank of the United States: Report of the Majority*, April 30, 1832, 285, https://fraser.stlouisfed.org/title/3622. This includes lists of the directors of the bank.

116. "Nation's Oldest Cotton Mill to Shut Down," *Washington Post*, September 3, 1947.

117. Savage Manufacturing Company indenture to John Savage, AACo, WSG 9, March 4, 1823, 244.

118. Edward Gray Mortgage with John Savage, AACo, WSG 9, November 29, 1834, 243.

119. Filby, *Savage, Maryland*, 13–14.

120. National Portrait Gallery, Smithsonian. John Savage by Thomas Sully. Object Number MD040022. Catalog of American Portraits. https://npg.si.edu/portraits/research/search.

121. D. Fitzhugh Savage Certificate of Death, Pennsylvania Historic and Museum Commission; Harrisburg, Pennsylvania; Death Certificates, 1906–1968; Certificate Number 92074. October 7, 1939.

122. John Savage Death Record. Michigan Department of Community Health, Division for Vital Records and Health Statistics; Lansing, Michigan. Death Records April 18, 1896; Savage Burial Vault, Ronaldson Cemetery.

123. Gerald Ueckermann prepared a detailed timeline of the mill ownership, which was very useful for this story.

124. 1850 Census: Mortality Statistics of the Seventh Census of the United States, 1855.

125. "Guilford, Howard Co, Md.," *Annapolis Maryland Republican and State Capital Advertiser*, July 27, 1878.

126. William C. Spelman, *Textile Manufactures' Directory of the United States, 1881*, 267.

127. George F. Swain, "Report on the Water-Power of the Middle Atlantic Water-shed," U.S. Decennial Census of 1880, June 1, 1882.

Chapter 5

128. The modern state of West Virginia was, in 1831, part of Virginia. It remained so until 1861, when it broke away from Virginia after the latter seceded from the federal Union.

129. Interstate Commerce Commission. 1918. Right-of-Way and Track Map. The B&O Railroad Company, Office of Valuation Engineer, Baltimore, Maryland. This map was purchased from the B&O Railroad Museum, Hays T. Watkins Research Library, Baltimore.

130. George Williams written interrogatory answers to Amos Williams vs. Savage Manufacturing Company, File No. 17898-12381-2, p. 29, June 1851, courtesy MSA.

131. Letter from George Williams to Amos Williams protesting the cost of the railroad bridge among other related expenses, MSA, File No. 17898-12381-1, February 4, 1835, courtesy MSA.

132. "Excavated Bridge Unearths Clues to State's History," *Baltimore Sun*, May 26, 1985.

133. "Completion of Branch Railroad," *Baltimore Sun*, January 19, 1888.

134. B&O Railroad Company. Form 6. List of Officers, Agents, Stations. Issued September 1, 1889. Purchased from B&O Railroad Historical Society in Eldersburg, Maryland.

135. The B&O Railroad Historical Society had several "Form 6" books for the following years after 1889: 1904, 1913, 1922, 1928 and 1948.

136. Interstate Commerce Commission. Finance Docket No. 6731. Abandonment of Part of Branch Line by Baltimore & Ohio Railroad. This covered a distance of two and a half miles. Issued March 21, 1928.

137. "B&O Washington Branch," Patuxent Branch Line, TrainWeb. org, http://www.trainweb.org/oldmainline/wasspur2.htm. This organization is a wonderful resource to our area history.

138. "Bollman Suspension Truss Bridge," Maryland Historical Trust Form HO-81 National Register of Historic Properties, https://mht. maryland.gov/nr/NRDetail.aspx?NRID=101. This bridge was also commemorated in 1966 as the first National Historic Civil Engineering Landmark by the American Society of Civil Engineers, and in 2000, it was named a National Historic Landmark by the National Park Service.

139. B&O Railroad, *23rd Annual Report of the Present and Directors to the Stockholders of the B&O Rail Road Company* (1849), 26; *24th Annual Report of the President and Directors to the Stockholders of the B&O Rail Road Company* (1850), 31–32.

140. Suspension Bridge. Wendel Bollman Patent No 8,624. January 6, 1852.

141. Robert M. Vogel, *The Engineering Contributions of Wendel Bollman,* Contributions from the Museum of History and Technology: Paper 36, Bulletin 240 (Washington, D.C.: Smithsonian Press, 1966).

142. John Doggett, *Railroads in New Jersey, Pennysylvania, Delaware and Maryland; Drawn and Engraved for Doggett's Railroad Guide & Gazetteer* (map; New York, 1848), https://www.loc.gov/item/98688351/.

143. Vogel, *Contributions of Wendel Bollman,* 99–103.

144. Interstate Commerce Commission (ICC) Railroad Valuation Records, Engineering Field Notes, Record Group 134, Valuation Section 18.2, Bridge Blueprintes, National Archives in College Park.

145. The newest Howard County site in the National Register of Historic Places, the Guilford Quarry Pratt Through Truss Bridge, is documented at the following link: https://mht.maryland.gov/secure/medusa/PDF/Howard/HO-349.pdf.

146. It was explained at the trailhead of Wincopin Trails in a poster by Howard County Department of Recreation and Parks that the Crib Dam "provided water power for the Savage Grist Mill, located 0.4 miles downriver."

147. The additional waterpower for Savage Mill was discussed in letters used as evidence in the 1852 Chancery Court proceedings of *Amos A.*

Williams vs. Savage Manufacturing Company. One of the letters discussing this, and the diversion from Hammond Branch, was an October 29, 1838 letter from Cumberland Dugan Williams to George Williams.

Chapter 6

148. Maryland State Archives Legacy of Slavery in Maryland, "Black Marylanders 1860: African American Population by County, Status & Gender," http://slavery.msa.maryland.gov/html/research/census1860.html.

149. The Presidential Election, "Official Vote of Maryland," *Baltimore Sun*, November 24, 1860.

150. Edward Breckinridge Lowndes, "What is Maryland, Anyway? Howard County," *Evening Sun* (Baltimore), August 22, 1922.

151. "An Act to Incorporate the Maryland State Colonization Society," 1831 Maryland Session Laws. V. 213, p. 426. Chapter 314. Passed March 14, 1832.

152. Ousmane K Power-Greene, *Against Wind and Tide: The African American Struggle Against the Colonization Movement* (New York: New York University Press, 2014), 18.

153. "An Act Relating to the People of Color in This State," 1831 Maryland Session Laws, V. 213, Chapter 281. Passed March 12, 1832, 343.

154. Ibid.

155. "An Act Relating to Free Negroes and Slaves," 1831 Maryland Session Laws, V. 213. Passed March 14, 1832, 445.

156. Maryland House of Delegates, "Report of the Committee on the Colored Population," Early State Records Online, Maryland State Archives, 136, February 9, 1842. This short and repugnant report was not unique on this issue.

157. Maryland State Archives, *Maryland Colonization Society Overview* (2012), 3. http://slavery.msa.maryland.gov/html/casestudies/mscs_overview.pdf.

158. Ibid.

159. Marlena Jareaux, Wayne Davis and Christine Bulbul, *Early Ellicott City Black History* (Columbia, MD: Howard County Lynching Truth & Reconciliation Inc., 2023).

160. The 1850 census is the first to provide the name, age and race of each individual living in a household. The Howard District reported separately for Elk Ridge Landing, Ellicott Mills, Howard, Lisbon, Poplar Spring, Savage and Sykesville.

161. The 1860 census added personal estate value to the forms and reported separately for Ellicott Mills (in District 2) and each of the five election districts.

162. Henry A. Penny Jr. and Fanny Penny Deed to the First Baptist Church Trustees, JHO 78, October 22, 1903, 18; Henry A. Penny Jr. and Fanny Penny Deed to Willis J. Carter, JHO 78, January 10, 1904, 257; Willis J. Carter and Mary W. Carter Mortgage to Henry A. Penny Jr., JHO 78, January 14, 1904, 407. Due to the early deaths of both Willis J. Carter and Henry A. Penny Jr., the mortgage was not released until March 31, 1914.

163. Henry A. Penny Sr. was a longtime Guilford resident from around 1850 until he died in 1903.

164. Nicholas Worthington of John, Last Will and Testament. September 13, 1845, 91–115.

165. Ibid.

166. Jody Frey, "Tracing the Settlement of Howard County, MD" (website), Google Earth maps of the original land patents made using the kml files for HoCo land patents at https://jsfecmd.info/FREAK/ HoCoFiles.html; 2017, updated 2021.

167. "Emancipation by Will," *Liberator* (Boston), December 5, 1845; "Noble Example," *Boston Recorder*, January 1, 1846.

168. Howard District Register of Wills (Accounts of Sale), 1840–1851, C3234-1. MSA, February 1, 1848. Researched and located by Marlena Jareaux, https://iamlouisa.com/judge-dorsey/.

169. 1850 census, Howard District of Anne Arundel County.

170. Ibid.

171. Martenet, Map of Howard County.

172. Nicholas Worthington, of John, Will, Codicils November 18–21, HoCo Wills, WG1, November 18, 1845, 91–115.

173. Last will and testament of Thomas Worthington of John, manumission record Augustus Collins aged about 22 years, witnessed by Charles W. Dorsey, April 12, 1852.

174. 1850 census, Howard District, AACo, Family Number 463, August 17, 1850, Augustus's parents and siblings lived here in 1850 and was HoCo District 5 (after becoming a county in 1851) in the 1860 census when they lived near Abraham Dorsey along old Guilford Road.

175. Michael Dresser, "150 Years Ago, the Bloodshed Started Here," *Baltimore Sun*, April 19, 2011.https://www.baltimoresun.com/maryland/ bs-md-pratt-street-riot-20110418-story.html. The words to "Maryland,

My Maryland" began as a poem written by Confederate James Ryder Randal in memory of his friend killed in the Baltimore Riot of 1861 and became a song of the Lost Cause. It was repealed as the state song of Maryland as of July 1, 2021.

176. "Plotting an Insurrection," *Baltimore Sun*, July 30, 1861.

177. Circuit Court of Howard County, September term 1861, "Presentment for raising insurrection," September 6, 1861.

178. Circuit Court of Howard County, September term 1861, "Presentment for resisting officer Welsh in the discharge of his duties," September 6, 1861.

179. Circuit Court of Howard County, September term 1861, request by Augustus Collins to court to move his case to an adjoining county for a fair trial. September 9, 1861.

180. "Circuit Court for Anne Arundel County," *Baltimore Sun*, January 28, 1862.

181. "Proceedings of the County Court," *Baltimore Sun*, January 24, 1862.

182. "Public Sale," *Baltimore Sun*, March 17, 1862. Announcement of the public sale of "a NEGRO MAN, named AUGUSTUS COLLINS" on March 18, "sentenced to be sold as a slave, for seven years, out of the State."

183. Enlistment in US Navy at Wilmington, DE. 1862, November 26th. Described as "bald, mulatto, 5' 5.5." Age 32.

184. Enlisted in the U.S. Navy at Washington, D.C., on "cruise of Gettysburg," September 23, 1875. This seemed to be a minor supply trip. He was listed as bald, 5'4.25", hazel-eyed and $44^8/_{12}$ years of age. Discharged at Norfolk, Virginia, on October 25, 1875.

185. Agnes Collins, widow of Augustus W. Collins, pension application and testimony. August 6, 1890. Deposition of July 26, 1892, has the most personal details. There were 143 pages of this pension application located in Fold3.com as Civil War pensioner's certificate number 11350.

186. Maryland Historical Trust. Ho-639 Howard's Family Homeplace for Free Slaves, 1994.

187. Mike Dwyre, "International Underground Railroad Month," Visit Howard County, Maryland, August 31, 2021, https://www.visithowardcounty.com/blog/post/harriet-tubman-the-simpsonville-freetown-legacy-trail/.

188. Pauline C. Moss and Levirn Hill, *Seeking Freedom—A History of the Underground Railroad in Howard County, Maryland* (Columbia: Howard County Center of African American Culture Inc., 2002), 29.

189. Michael Kammen, *Mystic Chords of Memory* (New York: Vintage, 1993), 626.

190. William Reynolds Jr. Trustee Deed to Jeremiah Wilson, 12 acres 100 sq perches, HoCo, WWW 28, April 8, 1868, 273; Jeremiah Wilson Deed to the Trustees of Locust Chappel—half acre, HoCo, WWW 29, August 19, 1869, 358.

191. Unpublished collection of personal research conducted by Beulah M. Buckner, in possession of Howard County Department of Recreation and Parks.

192. HO-639, "Howard's Family Homeplace for Free Slaves," Maryland Historical Trust, Crownsville, Maryland. This simple description of an alleged historic site is based on recollections and stories passed down, with the salient claims not able to be verified through fact-checking.

193. Moss and Hill, *Seeking Freedom*.

194. The National Archives in Washington, D.C.; NARA Microform Publication: M432; Title: Seventh Census of the United States, 1850; Record Group: Records of the Bureau of the Census; Record Group Number: 29.

195. "New Election Law," *Baltimore Sun*, March 21, 1901.

196. "Gorman Speaks—Talks on Negro Issue," *Baltimore Sun*, October 25, 1903.

197. Ibid.

198. "Is Gorman Night," *Baltimore Sun*, October 31, 1903.

199. "Gorman Hits Out," *Baltimore Sun*, October 27, 1905.

200. "Mr. Warfield's Speech of Acceptance at Mt. Airy," *Aegis & Intelligencer* (Bel Air, MD), October 2, 1903.

201. "For Amendment," *Baltimore Sun*, September 15, 1909.

202. "In Effect July First: On and After July First Colored People Must Ride Jim Crow Cars," *Baltimore Afro American Ledger*, June 25, 1904.

203. "Tells of Slave Life—Former Governor Warfield on Old Plantation Days," *Baltimore Sun*, April 13, 1912; "Edwin Warfield: Farmer and Financier," *Baltimore Sun*, January 22, 1911.

Chapter 7

204. *Report of the Principal of the State Normal School, Shewing the Condition of the Public Schools of Maryland, with the Reports of the County School Commissioners, for the Year Ending September 30, 1868* (Annapolis: George Colton, 1868), 5–7, 14.

205. *First Annual Report of the State Superintendent of Public Instruction Showing the Condition of the Public Schools of Maryland for the School Year Ending June 30ᵗʰ 1866* (Annapolis: Henry A. Lucas Printer), 64.

206. Elaine C. Everly, "Freedmen's Bureau Records: An Overview," *Federal Records and African American History* 29, no. 2 (1997): https://www.archives.gov/publications/prologue/1997/summer/freedmens-bureau-records.html.

207. U.S. Freedmen's Bureau, "Records Relating to School Buildings, Grounds and Supplies, 1865–1870." Freedmen's Bureau School Records were examined from 1864 through 1870, available from FamilySearch. Maryland and Howard County records were included in scattered monthly and other reports under the geographic area of the District of Columbia.

208. U.S. Freedmen's Bureau, "Teacher's Monthly School Report" for the Mission School, May 1870.

209. "John T.R.R. Carroll Found Dead. Was County Surveyor for Many Years and One of County's Picturesque Characters," *Ellicott City Times*, June 12, 1923.

210. HoCo Board of Education Meeting Minutes, April 24, 1865, 8; Benjamin Paul Ebersole, *A History of the Maryland State Teachers' Association*, Digital Repository at the University of Maryland (DRUM), 1964, https://drum.lib.umd.edu/handle/1903/19640.

211. Maryland State Board of Education, "Teacher's Pension Law," in *Thirty-Eighth Annual Report Showing Condition of the Public Schools in Maryland for the Year Ending July 31ˢᵗ, 1904* (1904), 59. Carroll is the eleventh name on the list and the first from Howard County to receive the first pension, offered on August 27, 1902.

212. "Howard County," *Baltimore Sun*, November 5, 1879

213. "The Complete Ticket," *Baltimore Sun*, June 20, 1907.

214. "John T.R.R. Carroll Found Dead."

215. "History of Asbury United Methodist Church, 1867 to 2017," Asbury Jessup United Methodist Church, http://asburyjessupumc.org/updating/.

216. Cornelius Mack and Wife Deed to the Trustees of Asbury Church, HoCo, JHO 59, 224, November 23, 1892; Marriage Licenses, Richard L. Carter and Dora E. Mack, *Baltimore Sun*, January 8, 1905.

217. *19ᵗʰ Annual Report of the State Board of Education for the Year Ending July 31, 1885*, 1886, 270; *32ⁿᵈ Annual Report of the State Board of Education for the Year Ending July 31, 1898*, 1899, 220.

218. HoCo Board of Education of meeting minutes, August 4, 1892.

219. "Maryland Matters—Affairs All Over the State," *Cumberland (MD) Daily Times*, December 13, 1884; "No Truth in the Lynching Story," *Baltimore Sun*, December 15, 1884.

220. "Douglas Day—The Famous Colored Man Speaks at Irving Park Camp," *Baltimore Sun*, August 20, 1891.

221. *35th Annual Report of the State Board of Education for the Year Ending July 31, 1901*, 1902, 38.

222. *Evening Capital* (Annapolis, MD), August 6, 1904.

223. W.P. Burrell and D.E. Johnson Sr., *Twenty-Five Years History of the Grand Fountain of the United Order of True Reformers, 1881–1905* (1919), 258, 446.

224. Ibid.

225. "History," Grand United Order of Odd Fellows. https://guoof.org/history/.

226. "Odd Fellows Name Fletcher as New Head," *Baltimore Afro American*, September 3, 1927.

227. "Hezekiah Brown Dies Suddenly at B.M.C.," *Baltimore Afro American*, September 15, 1928.

228. Howard County Lynching Truth & Reconciliation Inc. is a driver in Howard County for accurate history and public access to that history. This nonprofit organization is changing how history is viewed in the county. Please read about their continuing work on Hezekiah Brown: http://www.hocoltr.org/lynchings/rev-hezekiah-brown/.

229. Statement by Mr. Phillips in the 1907 *41st Annual Report of the State Board of Education* on the attitude of the county to educating Black children.

230. *40th Annual Report of the State Board of Education for the year ending July 31, 1906*, 1906, 285; HoCo School Board meeting minutes, May 2, 1905.

231. Names of the trustees were included in Howard County school board meeting minutes. Employment and presence in the area are from the U.S. Decennial Census for Howard County, Maryland, District 1 (1860), District 6 (1870), District 6 for the remaining years: Subdistrict 106 (1880), Subdistrict 0088 (1900), Subdistrict 0058 (1910), Subdistrict 0065 (1920), Subdistrict 0015 (1930) and Savage Subdistrict 14-12A (1940).

232. Ibid.

233. Find a Grave, "Jacob A. Coleman," First Baptist Church of Guilford Cemetery, 1881–1943, https://www.findagrave.com/memorial/143743408/jacob-a-coleman.

234. See chapter on Guilford's heyday.

235. HoCo School Board meeting minutes, May 18, 1920.

236. Holly Roose, "Rosenwald Fund Schools (1912–1932)," BlackPast, June 7, 2011, https://www.blackpast.org/african-american-history/rosenwald-fund-schools-1912-1932.

237. HoCo School Board meeting minutes, May 18, 1920.

238. HoCo School Board meeting minutes, January 4, 1922.

239. HoCo School Board meeting minutes, February 7, 1922.

240. *56th Annual Report to the Maryland State Board of Education for the Year Ending July 31, 1922*, table 58, 1922, 199.

241. Maryland Inventory of Historic Properties, HO-1058, https://mht.maryland.gov/secure/medusa/PDF/Howard/HO-1058.pdf.

242. HoCo School Board meeting minutes, April 7, 1953, 124, and October 3, 1950.

243. HoCo School Board meeting minutes, March 7, 1950; April 25, 1950; November 8, 1950, December 19, 1950.

244. HoCo School Board meeting minutes, September 8, 1952.

245. A March 2, 1954 letter from the county commissioners to the board of education of Howard County stating the school would open in September was presented at the April 6, 1954 school board meeting.

246. HoCo School Board meeting minutes, June 1, 1954, 202–3.

247. HoCo School Board meeting minutes, January 7, 1955, petition opposing desegregation.

248. HoCo School Board meeting minutes, August 16, 1955, 51–52.

249. HoCo School Board meeting minutes, February 9, 1965, 27, 30.

250. HoCo School Board meeting minutes, April 7, 1964, 157.

251. HoCo School Board meeting minutes, July 7, 1964, 204.

252. "Desegregation Recalled in School's Celebration," *Baltimore Sun*, November 18, 1994.

253. Kevin Dayhoff, "Remarks at Martin Luther King, Jr. Celebration by Allan H. Kittleman January 16, 2005," *Dayhoff Soundtrack* (blog), January 17, 2005, https://kevindayhoff.blogspot.com/2013/06/remarks-at-martin-luther-king-jr.html.

254. Board of Education of Howard County, "Proclamation: Apology for the Operation of a Racially Segregated School System," November 15, 2012.

255. Roger Sylvester Carter, Draft WWII Registration Card, October 16, 1940.

256. Lakeland High School opened in 1928. "Lakeland: Historic African American Community of College Park," *Route One Fun* (blog), April 3, 2020, https://www.routeonefun.com/lakeland-african-american-college-park/.

257. "Wanda Wilson Garcia Guilford Oral History Interview," with Joan Carter-Smith and Wayne Davis, posted by Friends of Guilford Industrial Historic District, YouTube, March 19, 2022, https://www.youtube.com/watch?v=EBkKG8VAeAM. "The children are watching."

258. Ibid.

259. Marilyn Miles, *The Carter Bus Company—Its Historical Significance in Howard County, Maryland*, University of Maryland Baltimore County Ronald McNair Scholars Program, 1999.

260. "Frederick Road Blocked," *Cumberland Evening Times*, July 18, 1945.

261. Miles, *Carter Bus Company*, 14; "Wanda Wilson Garcia Guilford."

262. Miles, *Carter Bus Company*, 15.

263. The Church of One Faith and One God Deed to Roger S. Carter and Agnes E. Carter, HoCo, CMP 642, 255, June 19, 1973.

264. "Advertisement. Ellicott City Howard County Historical Tours," *Baltimore Sun*, May 25, 1975; *Maryland Historical Magazine*, Spring 1977, 36.

265. "Roger S. Carter, Owner of Howard Bus Company," *Baltimore Sun*, February 22, 1984; Agnes Carter Deed to Howard County, Maryland, HoCo, MDR 3544, July 26, 1995, 25.

266. Miles, *Carter Bus Company*, 16.

267. "Carter Pioneers Rotary Club," *Baltimore Sun (HoCo Edition)*, November 15, 1987.

268. "Wanda Wilson Garcia Guilford."

269. "Roger Carter Portrait Unveiling," Howard County Government, October 15, 2022, https://www.flickr.com/photos/hocogov/albums/72177720302962324.

Chapter 8

270. "B. and O. Railroad Extension," *Baltimore Sun*, May 2, 1900.

271. "Guilford Quarry Railroad Completed," *Baltimore Sun*, April 15, 1901.

272. "Maryland Granite Company," *Baltimore Sun*, February 14, 1901.

273. "Realty and Building," *Baltimore Sun*, April 12, 1902.

274. *Stone: An Illustrated Magazine* 22 (1901), 145.

275. *Monumental News: A Monthly Journal of Monumental Art* 14, no. 6 (June 1902), 378.

276. Watson, *Granites*, 54–56.

277. Census records are available from 1900, 1910 and 1920 containing the names of the individuals who identified themselves as quarry workers.

278. "Special and Important Auction Sale," *Baltimore Sun*, July 11, 1917.

279. Freedmen's Bureau Bank Records—Albert Carter. Roll 27. Richmond, Virginia. June 21, 1870–June 29, 1874.

280. "Noted Men Gone to Their Reward," *Richmond Planet*, December 16, 1899.

281. 1880 U.S. Census, Henrico County, Virginia. Tuckahoe District, Supervisors District 3, Enumeration District 68. June 17, 1880, 28.

282. *Richmond Virginia City Directory*, 1891, 201.

283. "West End Notes," *Richmond Planet*, July 13, 1895.

284. Ibid.

285. Charles Carter Draft Registration, born Granite, MD, on August 28, 1896, June 5, 1918.

286. *Richmond Dispatch*, November 18, 1897. This is a notice of the sale of Willis J. Carter property.

287. "Good Man Passed Away—Mr. Albert Carter Met with a Fatal Accident," *Richmond Planet*, February 10, 1900.

288. 1900 Census. Baltimore County, Granite, Supervisors District 3, Enumeration District 23, Sheet 4, June 5, 1900.

289. Morse, Moss and Carter, unpublished family history, 1986.

290. Henry Penny Jr. and Wife Deed Trustees of the First Baptist Church of Guilford, HoCo, JHO 78, October 22, 1903, 18–19. Henry A. Penny Jr. and Wife Deed to Willis J. Carter, 13.25 acres, HoCo, JHO 78, January 10, 1904, 257–58.

291. HoCo School Board meeting minutes, 1905–1952.

292. Willis J. Carter gravestone located at First Baptist Church of Guilford Cemetery June 5, 1906; P. Cocco, Mary Ward and Eva Buiatti, "Occupational Risk Factors for Gastric Cancer: An Overview," *Epidemiologic Reviews* 18, no 2 (1996): 218–34.

293. Cornelison, Craft and Price, *History of Blacks*, 64, 71–73.

294. HoCo School Board meeting minutes, May 2, 1923.

295. U.S. Army Transport Service Arriving and Departing Passenger Lists, 1910–1939, Record Group Number: 92; Roll Number: 465; Sheet No. 2 Line 34. Camp Meade August Automatic Replacement Draft Co. No. 2 Infantry (Colored); Walter Carter, personnel communications with Carter family; Morse, Moss and Carter, unpublished family history; "Auto Drivers Hurt at Camp Meade," *Baltimore Afro American*, July 18, 1918.

296. U.S. National Cemetery Interment Control Forms, 1928–1962. Charles Carter, Died December 3, 1955. Baltimore National Cemetery. Section H. Lot 2611.

297. Morse, Moss and Carter, unpublished family history.

298. "Everybody Pleased. The Guilford Day Celebration a Big Success," *Ellicott City Times*, September 22, 1906.

299. "Mr. Mahool at Tourney. Goes to Guilford and Rides through Arches with Wife," *Baltimore Sun*, August 18, 1907.

300. "Politics at Guilford. But There Was Plenty of Other Things at Fine Picnic, 6,000 Persons Is the Estimate," *Baltimore Sun*, August 21, 1910.

301. "3,000 at Guilford Day. Great Event of Howard County Held at Ellicott City," *Baltimore Sun*, August 19, 1917.

302. "Picnic Season Over," *Ellicott City Times*, August 20, 1920. This was the last Guilford Day celebration.

303. "State Tax Delinquents. Guilford Day Association of Howard County," *Baltimore Sun*, March 19, 1921.

304. "Murder Mystery Near Solution," *Ellicott City Times*, August 10, 1922.

305. "Body of Slain Man Found in Tree Trunk J. Bernard Pattison Mysteriously Shot to Death," *Baltimore American*, May 19, 1922.

306. "Death of Pattison a Mystery," *Ellicott City Times*, May 26, 1922.

307. "Probe Fails to Solve Murder of Pattison. Inquest Is Held in Howard County Mystery," *Baltimore American*, May 27, 1922; State of Maryland Certificate of Death. Joseph Bernard Pattison, Date of Death May 11, 1922. Registration District No. 195, Burial at Bonnie Brae Cemetery May 20, 1922. SE43-003327.

308. "Affinities Arrested in Pattison Murder; Accuse Each Other," *Baltimore American*, August 6, 1922.

309. "Mrs. Pease 'Mugged' with Cronmiller," *Evening Sun (Baltimore)*, August 7, 1922.

310. "Intimates Admit Part in Murder," *Baltimore Sun*, August 6, 1922.

311. Howard County Criminal Docket, Criminals September Term, 1922, JHO3, 400, MSA T1037-1, 1922.

312. "Cronmiller Claims Woman Shot Pattison," *Evening Capital* (Annapolis), October 24, 1922.

313. Ibid.

314. "Letters of Cronmiller Reproach Mrs. Pease for Betrayal of Love," *Baltimore American*, October 25, 1922.

315. "Cronmiller Claims Woman Shot Patterson," *Evening Capital (Annapolis)*, October 24, 1922.

316. "Cronmiller Sentenced to Eighteen Years," *Ellicott City Times*, October 26, 1922.

317. "Mrs. Pease on Trial in Pattison Murder—Only Three Jurymen Out of First 23 Examined Are Chosen," *Evening Sun* (Baltimore), November 1, 1922.

318. *Midland Journal* (Rising Sun, MD), November 3, 1922; "Mrs. Pease Released—Reconciliation with Husband Follows Trial," *Baltimore Sun*, November 3, 1922.

319. North Carolina Marriage Records, Mary Reely Pease to Charlie P. Irby, Pasquotank, NC, October 8, 1959; Marybelle Pease Irby, Oak Hill Burial Park, Lakeland, Polk County, Florida, November 26, 1892. Parents listed confirmed her: Richard David Reely and Annie M. Reely. Courtesy of Find a Grave.

320. 1930 U.S. Census. William Cronmiller, Baltimore City, Maryland Penitentiary, Enumeration District 0149. Sheet 3A, April 4, 1930.

321. "Woman Slayer of Negro Chauffeur Seeks Parole," *Baltimore Sun*, January 22, 1929; "Ritchie Approves 35 Paroles, Pardon," *Baltimore Sun*, July 23, 1930; "Ritchie Gives Paroles to 24 MD Prisoners," *Daily Times* (Salisbury, MD), July 27, 1932.

322. 1940 U.S. Census. William Cronmiller. Laurel, Prince Georges County, MD. Enumeration District: 17-33; Page: 4B. Worked at the Navy Yard as a "molder helper."

323. William Carter Cronmiller, Ivy Hill Cemetery, Laurel, Prince Georges County, MD, Plot W220, September 18, 1945, Courtesy of Find a Grave.

324. June 3, 2015 message on Find a Grave.

Chapter 9

325. "Baldwin Hall Centennial Celebration," Carroll Baldwin Hall, https://www.carrollbaldwinhall.org/centennial-celebration.

326. Gideon White Deed to John Savage, White's Contrivance and Mill Land, AACo, WSG 9, 233, January 24, 1823.

327. Filby, *Savage, Maryland*, 12.

328. Amos A. Williams vs. Savage Manufacturing Co. Howard District. February 22, 1847. Petition to discover the accounts of SMC. MSA Accession No.: 17,898-12381-1/.

329. Votes and Proceedings of the House of the General Assembly of the State of Maryland, at December Session, 1821, 144.

330. Dixon Brown Deed to SMC. "Pinkstones Thicket," 50 acres, AACo, WSG 9, April 2, 1822, 622; Warner Warfield et al. Deed to SMC. "Warfields Range," 114 acres. AACo, WSG 9, April 8, 1822, 622.

331. Francis Simpson and Ephraim S. Gaither Deed to SMC. Venison Park and part of Brothers Partnership. 87 acres. AACo, WSG 9, July 3, 1822, 28.

332. Gideon White Deed to John Savage. January 24, 1823; SMC Mortgage to John Savage. AACo, WSG 9, 243, March 4, 1923. Mortgage for $20,000 including Venison Park, Brothers Partnership, Pinkstones Thicket, and Whites Contrivance.

333. Gideon White Deed to John Savage, January 24, 1823.

334. *North American Review* 20, no. 46 (January 1825), 128, https://www.jstor.org/stable/25109293.

335. Amos A. Williams vs. Savage Manufacturing Co. Howard District. February 22, 1847. Petition to discover the accounts of Savage Manufacturing Co. Accession No.: 17,898-12381-1/18 MSA S512-15-12185. Location: 1/39/4/. The chancery court case was decided in the September term, 1848.

336. Ibid. There are several hundred pages of documents in a file box associated with the discovery for this chancery court filing.

337. 1850 Census of Manufacturers. AACo, Maryland. Howard District.

338. Williams vs. Savage Manufacturing Co., High Court of Chancery of Maryland 1 Md. Ch. 306 (1848). September 1848.

339. Amos A. Williams vs SMC. Petition to discover.

340. McGrain, *Howard County Mills*, 87.

341. 1900 U.S. Census, Baltimore, Ninth District, First Precinct, June 15, 1900; World War I Draft Registration Card, San Diego County, California, September 12, 1918; *Merchants Record and Show Window: An Illustrated Monthly for Merchants, Displaymen, Advertising Men*, vol. 42 (Nickerson and Collins, June 1918), 12.

342. "Harry H. Heim Funeral Set," *Baltimore Sun*, February 1, 1953.

343. 1940 U.S. Census. Baltimore City, Maryland, Ward 9, Block 25, Enumeration District: 4-191, April 2, 1940; "Local Industrial Boom," *Evening Sun* (Baltimore), May 21, 1941; "Advertisement," *Baltimore Sun*, May 18, 1941.

344. "Yule Tree Balls Made Here by the Million," *Evening Sun* (Baltimore), December 8, 1944.

345. "Savage Factory Acquired by Harry Heim," *Evening Sun* (Baltimore), February 12, 1948.

346. SMC of HoCo Deed to Santa Novelties, Incorporated. HoCo, MWB 205, 0375. August 24, 1948.

347. "Half Year After Sale, Savage Starts to Look Like New Town," *Evening Sun* (Baltimore), August 18, 1948.

348. "5,000 Children Attend as Maryland Town Becomes 'Santa Heim,'" *Evening Star* (Washington, D.C.), December 12, 1948; "15,000 Take Part in Opening of Santa's 'All-Year Home,'" *Washington Post*, December 12, 1948.

349. "Year-Around Santa Project Just Fizzles," *Flint Journal*, December 6, 1951; "'Christmas Town' Man Faces Income-Tax Evasion Charges," *Baltimore Sun*, April 26, 1949; "'Santa' Heim Fined $100. Convicted of Failing to File State Income-Tax Return," *Baltimore Sun*, June 16, 1949.

350. Harry Heim Sr. and His Wife Nellie Heim Deed to National Store Fixture Co, Inc. October 2, 1950. HoCo, MWB 220, 84; "Public Auctions—Office of the Collector of Internal Revenue Baltimore, Maryland," *Baltimore Sun*, April 29, 1951.

351. "Harry H. Heim Funeral Set," *Baltimore Sun*, February 1, 1953.

352. National Industries (formerly National Store Fixture Co. Inc.) Deed to Ephraim and Samuel Winer, Co-Partners in Savage Company, HoCo, WHH 436, 0055, May 27, 1965.

353. Certificate of Incorporation of Carroll Baldwin Memorial Institute, Inc. State of Maryland. June 23, 1922. Courtesy of Maryland State Archives.

354. Savage, *Prince Georges Enquirer and Southern Maryland Advertiser* (Upper Marlboro, MD), December 15, 1922).

355. "Offered Posts on Board," *Baltimore Sun*, December 28, 1922.

356. "Library Association Formed," *Baltimore Sun*, October 10, 1920.

357. "Contract for the Construction of the Carroll-Baldwin Memorial at Savage," *Baltimore Sun*, May 26, 1921.

358. *Maryland Library Notes* 1, no. 2 (Towson, MD: Maryland Public Library Commission, February 1922), 3.

359. *Official Opinions of the Attorney General of Maryland*, June 14, 1922, 258.

360. Florence A. Huxley, *The American Library Directory 1927* (New York: R.R. Bowker, 1927), 85.

361. Maryland Public Library Commission, *Biennial Report for the Years 1912 and 1913* (Baltimore: Waverly Press, 1913), 20.

362. Ibid.

363. "Library at Savage Has Opened Again," *Ellicott City Times*, February 29, 1956.

364. Lease of Library Quarters. Board of Library Trustees meeting minutes, July 21, 1966.

365. HoCo Library Request for Proposal for Automated Library Circulation System, Board of Library Trustees meeting minutes, April 1979.

366. "Council to Trim Budget Elsewhere to Free Money for HCC," *Baltimore Sun*, May 19, 1987.

367. "Historical Timeline," HCPL, https://hclibrary.org/about-us/history/timeline/.

368. Cornelison, Craft and Price, *History of Blacks*, 61–62.

369. "Savage, Maryland," History and Social Justice website, 2022, https://justice.tougaloo.edu/sundowntown/savage-md/.

370. Cornelison, Craft and Price, *History of Blacks*, 61.

371. 1870 U.S. Census. HoCo, Maryland. District 6. Post Office Savage. June 24, 1870, page 45, Harriet Watkins; June 25, 1870, page 50, Augusta Boston.

372. Reviewing each census between 1880 and 1940 showed there were no Black or Mulatto (the only two options other than White) people living there. Areas on Guilford Road considered Guilford or Jessup were excluded.

373. Justice Map. Visualize race and income for your community and country. 2020 Early Release, 2022. https://www.justicemap.org/2020/.

374. SMC Deed to Board of Education, HoCo, HBN 114, 298, October 2, 1921.

375. SMC Deed to Board of Education, HoCo, BM Jr. 159, 130, December 20, 1937.

376. "Minstrel Show in Savage Friday, June 9," *Ellicott City Times*, June 2, 1922.

377. Olde Time Minstrel Show. December 7 and 8, 1956, and the Second Annual Olde Time Minstrel Show. Community Hall Savage Maryland, sponsored by Carroll Baldwin Memorial Association.

378. "Klan Leaflets in Howard Fire Station Prompt Call for Inquiry," *Baltimore Sun*, March 22, 1983.

379. "Howard Held Lax on Racist Acts," *Baltimore Sun*, November 2, 1983.

380. "Racist Vandals Forcing Black Family to Move," *Evening Sun* (Baltimore), December 12, 1985.

381. "Community Leaders in Savage Deny Racism, Blame Incidents on Quarrels," *Baltimore Sun*, December 17, 1985.

382. Justice Map, 2022.

383. "Carroll Baldwin Hall's Commitment to Diversity, Equity, and Inclusion," 2022, https://www.carrollbaldwinhall.org/diversity-equity-and-inclusion.

Chapter 10

384. Robert Moxley, "Land Acquisition: The Realtor's Perspective," in *Creating a New City—Columbia, Maryland*, edited by Robert Tennenbaum (Columbia: Partners in Community Building and Perry Publishing, 1996), 23–31.

385. "900 Acres of Howard Farm Land Purchased," March 25, 1963, *Evening Sun* (Baltimore).

386. Howard County land records were successfully searched once a date and company name was acquired per Tennenbaum 1996.

387. "14,000 Acres in Howard to Be Developed," *Baltimore Sun*, October 30, 1963.

388. "History—Explore Columbia," Columbia Association, Columbia Archives, 2018, https://www.columbiaassociation.org/explore-columbia/history/.

389. 2020 U.S. Census. QuickFacts—Columbia Census Designated Place, Maryland.

390. "Memoranda of Action of State Roads Commission of Maryland," by chairman and director Jerome B. Wolff, February 5, 1968, Howard County SRC (State Roads Commission).

391. *HoCo General Plan.* HoCo Planning Commission, 1960, 22; *A Supplement to the Text of the Howard County General Plan to Guide the Construction of New Towns, New Communities and Large-Scale Neighborhoods* (HoCo Planning Commission), adopted on May 17, 1965.

392. "Roads Unit to Offer Land to Howard County Families," *Baltimore Sun*, June 11, 1967.

393. "Progress Spells Death for Old Rural Town," *Columbia Villager*, February 16, 1972. Available at the Columbia Archives.

394. Ibid.

395. See the stories in this chapter on "Alternate Realities."

396. "Beaula Moore Oral History Interview 10-22-2020," with Joan-Carter Smith and Wayne Davis, posted by Friends of Guilford Industrial Historic District, YouTube, October 22, 2020, Guilford Oral History Project, https://www.youtube.com/watch?v=Igf8xPqmnxI.

397. See story in this chapter for "Recommissioning the Patuxent Branch Railroad."

398. Columbia Archives. There are dozens of pieces of communication to and from Rouse company officials, including James Rouse, from December 1966 through April 1969 on the issue of building railway access to their industrial site to attract potential buyers.

399. Ibid.
400. "This Week in Columbia History: General Electric Announced Start of Work on New Columbia Plant," *Baltimore Sun*, June 7, 2017.
401. USEPA. 2022 Hazardous Waste Cleanup: Former Appliance Park East (General Electric Company) in Columbia, Maryland.
402. "Columbia Gateway Innovation District," Howard County Economic Development Authority, https://hceda.org/innovation-startups/columbia-gateway-innovation-district/.
403. HoCo by Design. 2022. Gateway. HoCo by Design is the public process for updating the ten-year general plan.
404. West Virginia Corporation Report of the Secretary of State. 1919. March 1, 1907, to March 1, 1909. P. 130. Guilford Granite and Stone Company (non-resident). Issued May 25, 1901, expires May 25, 1957.
405. Deed Between Guilford Granite and Stone Company, a West Virginia Corporation and Guilford Granite and Stone, Co., a Maryland Corporation. Howard County RHM 342, p. 0508, June 18, 1959.
406. Donald Lee Sherman and Marjorie S. Sherman Deed to Guilford Granite and Stone Company. Howard County, WHH 442, p. 0747, September 23, 1965.
407. "Quarry Hearings Goes On, and On, and On," *Ellicott City Times*, September 22, 1965.
408. "Quarrying Firm Is Denied Permit," *Baltimore Sun*, February 16, 1966.
409. Articles of Merger of Percon Inc., Howard-Montgomery Crushed Stone Inc. and Guilford Granite and Stone Company merging into Contee Sand and Gravel Company Inc., HoCo, CMP 1464, 708. March 31, 1967.
410. "'Appropriate Action' Promised in Arundel Case; Contee Up," *Howard County Times*, December 11, 1969.
411. "Rock Quarry Hearing Held," *Baltimore Sun*, December 31, 1969.
412. "Arundel Corporation Seeks to Continue Illegal Quarry," *Baltimore Sun*, April 3, 1970.
413. "Contee Petition Returned to Appeals Board," *Howard County Times*, April 27, 1970.
414. "'Great America' Park Here in '74," *Howard County Times*, January 27, 1972.
415. "CHAMP vs CRAMP: Chump Insurance Plan?," *Evening Sun* (Baltimore), April 26, 1972.
416. "Marriott Park Is Rejected by Howard Board," *Baltimore Sun*, September 23, 1972.

417. "More Than 60 Lodge Protests Against Proposed Landfill Sites," *Howard County Times*, January 26, 1977.

418. "No Surprise at Landfill Meeting. Six Possible Sites Detailed, None Chosen," *Howard County Times*, January 12, 1977.

419. "Marriottsville Is Chosen as Site for New Landfill," *Howard County Times*, February 9, 1977.

420. "Marriott Theme Park Site Sought," *Baltimore Sun*, March 2, 1977.

421. "Zoning Shift for Marriott Park Proposed," *Baltimore Sun*, June 15, 1977.

422. "Fighting Marriott Once Again," *Baltimore Sun*, August 8, 1977.

423. "Marriott Park Loses in Howard," *Baltimore Sun*, October 4, 1977.

424. "Marriott to Sell Last Theme Park," *Baltimore Sun*, April 27, 1984.

Chapter 11

425. George Norbury Mackenzie, *Colonial Families of the United States of America*, vol. 6 (New York: Grafton Press, 1917), 278–81.

426. John Carroll Marriage to Eliza Isaac. "Maryland Marriages, 1666–1970," FamilySearch database.

427. John Carroll Will. AACo Wills 1828–1847 vol. 40—image 44 of 304; December 10, 1829.

428. Ibid.

429. John G. Proud Deed to William Henry and Charles Carroll. AACo, WSG 15, March 1, 1830, 299–301.

430. 1830. Census Place: District 5, Anne Arundel, Maryland; Series: M19; Roll: 53; Family History Library Film: 0013176, 167. Accessed through Ancestry.com on April 4, 2020.

431. 1832. Benjamin Marlow and Eliza Carroll Marriage Record. "Maryland Marriages, 1666–1970," FamilySearch database.

432. 1850. Census Place: Berry's, Montgomery County, Maryland. Series Number: M432, Roll 295, page 352a. Benjamin Marlow is listed with his wife, Mary (Eliza's sister), along with Sarah E. Marlow (fifteen), presumed to be his daughter with Eliza (b. 1835).

433. Orphans Court of AACo, Wills 1828–1847. TTS No. 40, image 181 of 304. October 18, 1838.

434. 1840 Census. District 2, Baltimore, Maryland. Roll: 162; Page: 67.

435. David Carroll Account Book. H. Furlong Baldwin Library, Maryland Center of History and Culture. MS 0200. 1838.

436. 1840. Benjamin Marlow and Mary Ann Isaac Marriage Record. "Maryland Marriages, 1666–1970," FamilySearch database. Note: His middle initial was erroneously recorded here with an *R*; 1840 Census. District 2, Baltimore, MD. Roll: 162, 67.

437. 1860 Census. District 1, HoCo, MD. Elk Ridge Landing Post Office. November 14, 1860, 71.

438. 1870 Census. District 6, HoCo, MD. Savage Post Office, June 6, 1870, 8.

439. Mackenzie, *Colonial Families*, 281.

440. *Genealogical and Biographical Record of the Leading Families of Baltimore City and Baltimore County Maryland* (Chapman Publishing, New York, 1897), 304.

441. The headstone for Thomas Lemuel Carroll reads, "In memory of Thomas Lemuel son of David & Ann Carroll who departed this life July 29th, 1836, age 6 months & 22 days." The birth date of January 7 is calculated from 6 months and 22 days before Thomas died.

442. George Washington Howard, *The Monumental City, Its Past History and Present Resources* (Baltimore, 1873), 667–70.

443. "Savage Cotton Factory," *Baltimore Patriot & Mercantile Advertiser*, December 27, 1828; "Savage Cotton Factory," *Daily Richmond Whig*, May 12, 1829.

444. David Carroll Account Book, 1828–39; records of apprenticeships at Savage. MS 0200, MCHC.

445. Notice of the dissolution of the copartnership of the firm David Hack & Company from Daniel Hack and Amos A. Williams. *Baltimore Patriot and Mercantile Advertiser*, June 14, 1831; "Machinist Wanted" advertisement by Daniel Hack at Accoquan [*sic*], Virginia, *Baltimore Patriot and Mercantile Advertiser*, July 7, 1831.

446. David Carroll and Ann Elizabeth Aylor Marriage. October 12, 1833. Baltimore County Maryland Indexes. (Marriage Licenses Baltimore, Male Index.) Number 539, S1398-22.

447. Thomas Lemuel Carroll headstone.

448. "A Millionaire's Will," *Baltimore Sun*, August 10, 1881.

449. The records and notes of Beulah Buckner are in the possession of the Howard County Department of Recreation and Parks and are available for review on request.

450. Organizations that visited the cemetery suggesting African American burial throughout include Maryland State Highway Administration, Preservation Howard County, Coalition to Protect Maryland Burial

Sites and Smithsonian Environmental Research Group, as well as several individuals, including archaeologists and cemetery experts.

451. Although Fold3 is a subscription service, it has an incredible amount of information on the military records of hundreds of thousands of people. This record was hard to find due to Mr. Wyman going by "Frank" at times. His wife filed a pension request that recorded his death date and brief service in the Civil War. This information confirmed what was written on the grave marker.

452. Several newspaper articles covered this 1880 story, including ones in the *Washington Evening Star* on July 7, 8 and 9 and October 23 and the *Baltimore Sun* on July 9. Coverage of the lawsuit and settlement occurred in 1881 (*Baltimore Sun*, June 30) and 1882 (*Baltimore Sun*, April 14 and 15).

453. See *Baltimore Sun* and *Washington Evening Star* from August 7 and 8 of 1900, with the formal name change reported by the *Evening Star* on September 4.

454. The *Evening Star* covered the widow's pension claim on January 22, 1910, and the story about her 1927 death in its June 23 and 25 editions.

Selected Bibliography

Cornelison, Alice, Silas E. Craft Sr. and Lillie Price. *History of Blacks in Howard County, Maryland*. Columbia, MD: HoCo NAACP, 1986.

Filby, Vera Ruth. *Savage, Maryland*. Savage Civic Association, Savage, MD: P.W. Filby and V.R. Filby, 1965.

Griffith, Dennis. *Map of the State of Maryland Laid Down from an Actual Survey of All the Principal Waters, Public Roads and Divisions of the Counties Therein[…] June 20, 1794*. Philadelphia: J. Vallance, 1795. https://lccn.loc.gov/76693265.

Jareaux, Marlena, Wayne Davis and Christine Bubal. *Early Ellicott City Black History*. Columbia, MD: Howard County Lynching Truth & Reconciliation Inc., 2023.

Martenet, Simon J. *Martenet's Map of Howard County, Maryland: Drawn Entirely from Actual Surveys*. Baltimore: John Schofield, 1860. https://www.loc.gov/item/2002624032/.

———. *Martenet's Map of Maryland: Including the District of Columbia, a Sketch of Delaware, and a Portion of Northern and Eastern Virginia Showing Some of the Most Interesting Localities of the Late War*. Baltimore: Schmidt & Trowe, 1865. https://lccn.loc.gov/94681799.

Mathews, Edward B. "An Account of the Character and Distribution of Maryland Building Stones." In *Maryland Geological Survey*, vol 2. Baltimore: Johns Hopkins Press, 1898.

———. *The Counties of Maryland: Their Origin, Boundaries, and Election Districts*. HoCo: Baltimore: Johns Hopkins Press, 1907.

McGrain, John. *The Molinography of Maryland: A Tabulation of Mills, Furnaces, and Primitive Industries—Howard County Mills*. 1976. https://msa.maryland. gov/megafile/msa/speccol/sc4300/sc4300/000005/000000/000010/ unrestricted/howard%20county%20chapter.pdf.

———. *The Molinography of Maryland*. 2007. http://speccol.msa.maryland. gov/pages/speccol/collection.aspx?speccol=4300.

Tyson, Martha Ellicott. *A Brief Account of the Settlement of Ellicott's Mills: With Fragments of History Therewith Connected, Nov 3, 1870*. Baltimore: J. Murphy, 1981.

Vogel, Robert M. *The Engineering Contributions of Wendel Bollman*. Paper 36, Bulletin 240: Contributions from the Museum of History and Technology. Smithsonian Institution, 1966.

Warfield, Joshua Dorsey. *The Founders of Anne Arundel and Howard Counties, Maryland*. Baltimore: Kohn and Pollock, 1905.

Watson, Thomas Leonard. *Granites of the Southeastern Atlantic States*. U.S. Geological Survey Bulletin 426, 1910.

About the Authors

Photo by Sergio Almirez Photography.

Nathan S. Davis is the on-site manager of the Baltimore and Ohio Ellicott City Station Museum, operated by the Howard County Department of Recreation and Parks. A resident of Columbia, Maryland, for most of his life, Nathan has a history degree from the University of Maryland, Baltimore County, only ten minutes from his museum. He has devoted countless hours to researching Howard County history for professional and personal interest.

Wayne S. Davis is a retired federal government environmental scientist and researcher who began his career writing about environmental history before developing a more recent interest in local history. He promotes research and access to accurate local history, in part by hosting a Facebook group and a website and publishing local articles.